CHEMISTRY

FOR QUEENSLAND

UNITS 3 & 4

STUDENT WORKBOOK

CAROLYN DRENEN

Oxford University Press is a department of the University of Oxford.
It furthers the University's objective of excellence in research,
scholarship, and education by publishing worldwide. Oxford is a registered
trademark of Oxford University Press in the UK and in certain other
countries.

Published in Australia by
Oxford University Press
Level 8, 737 Bourke Street, Docklands, Victoria 3008, Australia.

First published 2019
1st Edition

Reprinted 2020, 2023 (twice)

ISBN 9780190320430

Edited by Penny Drago
Typeset by Newgen KnowledgeWorks Pvt. Ltd., Chennai, India
Proofread by Jocelyn Hargrave
Printed in India by Manipal Technologies Limited

Disclaimer
Indigenous Australians and Torres Strait Islanders are advised that this publication may include images or names of people now deceased.

Links to third party websites are provided by Oxford in good faith and for information only. Oxford disclaims any responsibility for the materials contained in any third party website referenced in this work.

CONTENTS

C2H4

Chemistry for Queensland Units 3 & 4 Student workbook is designed to help students succeed in their internal and external assessments. Each activity is supported with an engaging design, full-colour diagrams and answers at the back of the book.

Data drill
Activities that help students develop the key skills in analysis and interpretation required for the data test.

Experiment explorer
Tasks to support the modification of a practical as required in the Student experiment.

Research review
Activities that allow students to practise evaluating a claim and identify credible sources for the Research investigation.

Internal assessment support
This workbook includes a practice Data test, Student experiment and Research investigation to help students with their Units 3 & 4 internal assessments.

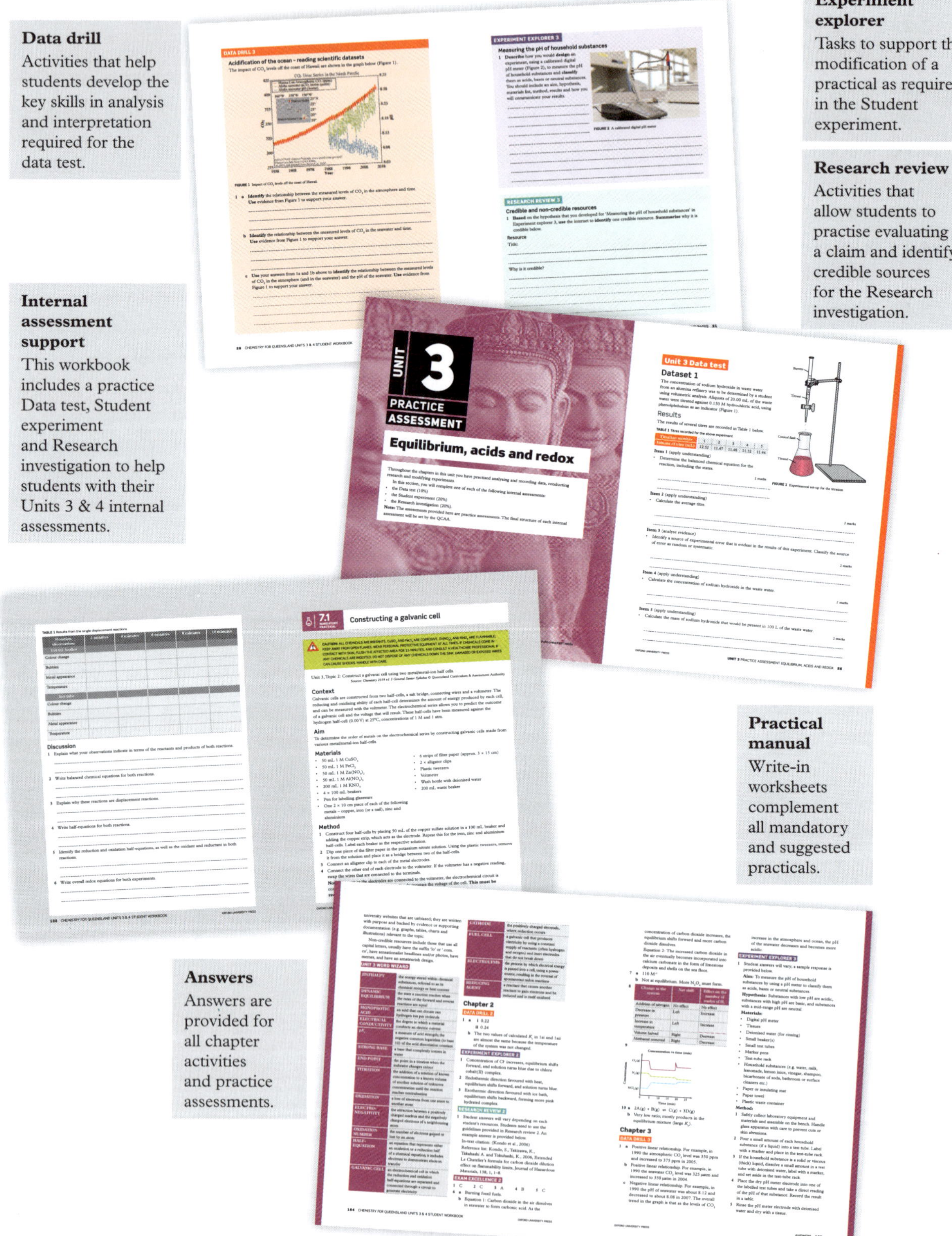

Practical manual
Write-in worksheets complement all mandatory and suggested practicals.

Answers
Answers are provided for all chapter activities and practice assessments.

ACKNOWLEDGEMENTS

The author and the publisher wish to thank the following copyright holders for reproduction of their material.

Chapter 1: Shutterstock, 3.4, chapter opener.

Chapter 2: Alamy/Paul Kennedy, unit 3 opener/ Martin Valigursky, chapter 2 opener.

Chapter 3: NOAA, 1.1; Shutterstock, 1.2, chapter opener.

Chapter 4: Alamy/Ian Redding, chapter 4 opener.

Chapter 5: Alamy/Taras Vyshnya, chapter 5 opener.

Chapter 6: Alamy/Stephanie Jackson, chapter 6 opener.

Chapter 7: Shutterstock, chapter 7 opener.

Chapter 8: Alamy/Paul Kennedy, unit 3 practice assessment opener; Shutterstock, chapter 8 opener, unit 3.1a, unit 3.1b.

Chapter 9: Science Photo Library/Volker Steger, unit 4 opener, Shutterstock, 9.1, chapter 9 opener.

Chapter 10: Shutterstock 10.1, chapter 10 opener.

Chapter 11: Alamy/Tim Gainey, chapter 11 opener; Shutterstock, 11.1.

Chapter 12: Shutterstock, chapter 12 opener, 12.1.

Chapter 13: Alamy/Tim Graham, chapter 13 opener, 13.1.

Chapter 14: Shutterstock, chapter 14 opener.

Chapter 15: Shutterstock, chapter 15 opener.

Chapter 16: Alamy/All Canada Photos, unit 4.1; Science Photo Library/Volker Steger, unit 4 practice assessment opener; Shutterstock, chapter 16 opener.

Chapter 17: Shutterstock, 10.2.1, chapter 17 opener.

This syllabus forms part of a new senior assessment and tertiary entrance system in Queensland. Along with other senior syllabuses, it is still being refined in preparation for implementation in schools from 2019. For the most current syllabus versions and curriculum information, please refer to the QCAA website www.qcaa.qld.edu.au pp. 34-5, 41, 42-3, 74, 96, 112, 136, 162-3, 188, 217, 250-1, 274-5, 298, 322, 342, 360, 392, 398.

Every effort has been made to trace the original source of copyright material contained in this book. The publisher will be pleased to hear from copyright holders to rectify any errors or omissions.

CHAPTER

1 Chemistry toolkit

The Chemistry toolkit is a resource for students to refer to while they are working through the activities and practicals in this workbook. It introduces the use of cognitive verbs and provides students with detailed information on how to answer each question. Cognitive verbs are bolded in each activity to highlight them for students.

The three internal assessments are explained in detail in the toolkit and each have an activity included to practice skills required for that assessment. The Data test (IA1) is worth 10% of the total student's mark and is completed in Unit 3. The Student experiment (IA2) is worth 20% and is also completed in Unit 3. The Research investigation (IA3) is worth 20% of the total student's mark and is completed in Unit 4.

CHAPTER CHECKLIST

Read this checklist before you complete this chapter's activities, then return to it to check your understanding before your assessments.

Once you have completed this chapter, you can use the 'I can …' statements to assess and rate your understanding of the topics covered by ticking the appropriate box in the 'rating column'.

I can …	Confidently	Partially	Not really
… respond to questions using cognitive verbs.			
… explain the requirements of the Unit 3 Data test.			
… explain the requirements of the Unit 3 Student experiment.			
… explain the requirements of the Unit 4 Research investigation.			
… find the necessary documentation for my assessments.			

1.1 Responding to cognitive verbs

In assessment tasks and examinations, you will encounter cognitive verbs. These verbs are 'task words' that will provide information on what is expected to answer a question.

It is important to understand the difference between task words. For example, a question that asks you to 'compare' is different from a command asking you to 'contrast'. One requires you to show similarities and differences, whereas the other only asks you show the differences.

If you understand exactly what a cognitive verb is asking for, then you can provide exactly what the examiner is looking for. Examiners want to give students marks but can only do so if students provide the correct information. For example, if a question asks you to **analyse** some data, you will not receive full marks if you only describe the data but do not analyse the data.

Table 1 is a list of cognitive verbs that you might encounter in your assessments. (A full list of the cognitive verbs is available on the *Chemistry for Queensland Units 3 & 4* Student obook assess).

TABLE 1 Cognitive verbs used in assessments

Cognitive verb	Definition	Sample question
Apply	use knowledge and understanding in response to a given situation or circumstance; carry out or use a procedure in a given or particular situation	**Apply** your knowledge of photosynthesis to explain how algae receive their energy.
Calculate	determine or find (e.g. a number, answer) by using mathematical processes; obtain a numerical answer showing the relevant stages in the working; ascertain/determine from given facts, figures or information	**Calculate** the mean for the provided dataset.
Compare	display recognition of similarities and differences and recognise the significance of these similarities and differences	**Compare** a strong and weak acid.
Describe	give an account (written or spoken) of a situation, event, pattern or process, or of the characteristics or features of something	**Describe** molar mass.
Determine	establish, conclude or ascertain after consideration, observation, investigation or calculation; decide or come to a resolution	**Determine** the molar mass of a pure substance if 3.5 moles of the substance has a mass of 59.584 g.
Explain	make an idea or situation plain or clear by describing it in more detail or revealing relevant facts; give an account; provide additional information	**Explain** why it is impossible for the percentage yield to be 109%.
Identify	distinguish; locate, recognise and name; establish or indicate who or what someone or something is; provide an answer from a number of possibilities; recognise and state a distinguishing factor or feature	**Identify** the range of values suggested by the measurement 10.3 ± 0.8 seconds.
Justify	give reasons or evidence to support an answer, response or conclusion; show or prove how an argument, statement or conclusion is right or reasonable	**Justify** why an absorption or emission spectrum is referred to as a fingerprint of an element.

Source: *QCAA Chemistry 2019 v1.3 General Senior Syllabus* © Queensland Curriculum & Assessment Authority

1.2 Data test

The Data test is a one-hour exam that includes 2–4 datasets (see Figure 1). This data may be qualitative, such as a statement of whether a reaction occurred or not, or it may be quantitative, such as the final concentrations of compounds in an equilibrium system at different temperatures. The types of questions will include short-response items (with single words or sentence responses) up to short-paragraph responses (fewer than 50 words). There will also be calculation-type questions, as well as questions requiring interpretation of datasets. For this task, 10 minutes of reading time at the beginning and 60 minutes of writing time will be allowed.

A graphics calculator is allowed. A chemical formula and data book is also permitted. Concentrate on how to use the formulas, constants and other information provided, rather than memorising this material.

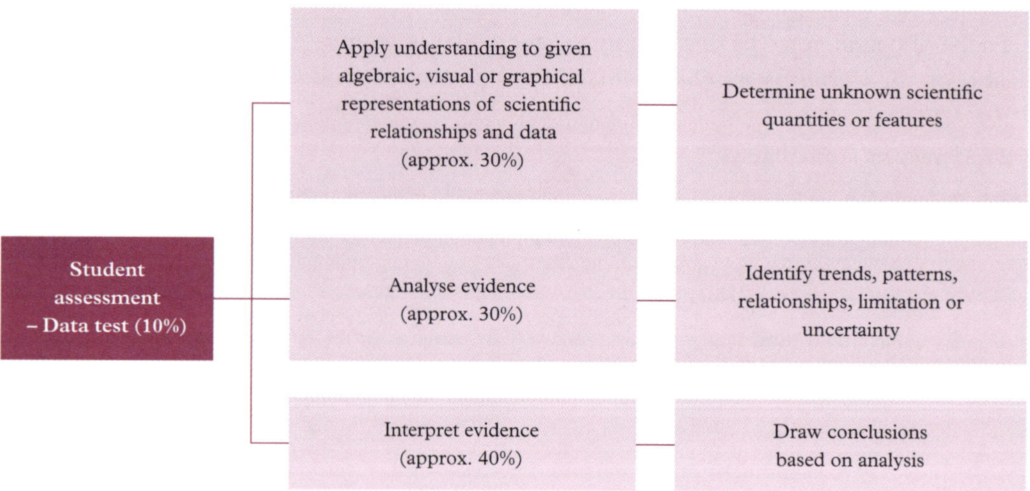

FIGURE 1 A graphical outline of the components of the Data test.

Key tips:

- Read the questions carefully. Be particularly wary of reading a question and assuming it is identical to something that you have seen before, only to realise the error when it is too late to fix.
- Do not state a conclusion without also outlining the evidence used to reach that conclusion. Watch out for giving evidence that is merely the conclusion stated in a different way; for example, 'The reaction was exothermic, because heat was given out', or 'Acid A is a stronger acid than acid B because it has a lower pK_a'.
- Mention any limits on the degree of certainty with which conclusions were drawn, if these exist. If certain assumptions need to be made to reach a conclusion, then state these assumptions; for example, 'It is assumed that the reaction solution was maintained at the same temperature throughout the solution'.

DATA DRILL 1

Identifying trends in data

A student conducted a redox laboratory experiment that simulated the measurement of blood glucose levels in body fluids, using a calorimeter, glucose ($C_6H_{12}O_6$) solutions, potassium permanganate ($KMnO_4$), deionised water and a sulfuric acid catalyst (H_2SO_4).

A series of glucose solutions of known concentrations were prepared and reacted with a set volume of a standard solution of $KMnO_4$ (and H_2SO_4 catalyst) in cuvettes of 3 mL volume. Each filled cuvette was placed in the calorimeter, and the extent of the reaction was measured by the percent absorbance of the colour change (from pink to colourless) as the permanganate ions were reduced to manganese ions. The raw data obtained from this experiment is given in Table 2.

TABLE 2 Raw data obtained from the experiment with glucose solutions

Sample	Glucose concentration (%)	Measured absorbance (%)
1	0	0.00
2	2	0.38
3	4	0.33
4	6	0.42
5	8	0.20
6	10	0.33
7	12	0.27

1 a **Describe** the purpose of using deionised water in this experiment.

b **Construct** the half-equation for the permanganate ions reducing to manganese ions.

c **Construct** a graph of the data in Table 1 with appropriate labels. **Identify** the relationship between glucose concentration and measured absorbance.

Study tip

If you find it hard to identify a relationship between a set of data draw a 'line of best fit' to help you to identify a data pattern.

1.3 Student experiment

The Student experiment is quite different from the other assessment items because it requires the collection, analysis and synthesis of primary data (see Figure 1). You must plan and carry out experiments to generate the data that you will then use to answer a question or to confirm (or reject) a hypothesis related to chemical equilibrium systems or oxidation and reduction. You will do this over a period of 10 hours of class time, so it will be important to plan a timeline for the project. Remember to allow time for the things that won't go according to plan, or will take longer than expected.

To plan the experiment, you will need to research and think about how to conduct the experiment. You will need to be flexible to adapt the experiment as you identify challenges. Students can sometimes be frustrated that experiments do not work properly the first time or give unclear results. Part of the learning process required is to learn how to trouble-shoot, to think clearly about what might be going wrong and to adjust the experiment accordingly. This may require going back and redoing experiments. Spending adequate time at the research and planning phase may enable some missteps to be avoided.

You then need to communicate the experimental data, results, findings and conclusion. This may be in a written format, such as a scientific report, of 1500–2000 words, or in a different format, such as a scientific poster with an oral presentation of 9–11 minutes. Not all aspects of the report are weighted equally (see Figure 3). Tips on how to write a high-quality scientific report can be found in the *Chemistry for Queensland Units 3 & 4* Student book.

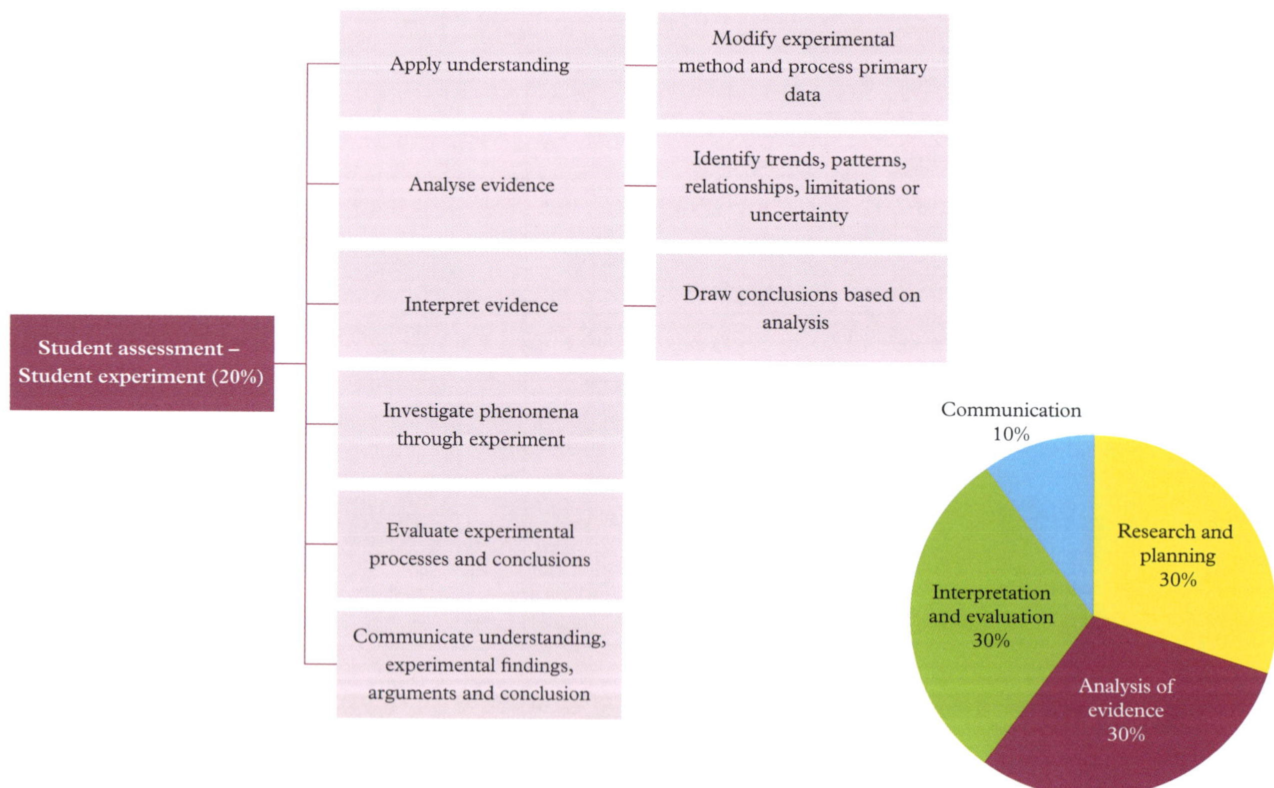

FIGURE 2 A graphical summary of the Student experiment

FIGURE 3 The mark breakdown of the elements in the Student experiment

EXPERIMENT EXPLORER 1

Determining acid strength by measuring conductivity

1 **Describe** how you would **design** an experiment to measure the electrical conductivity of acid solutions using the following apparatus: a multimeter water tester (Figure 4), glassware and acid solutions. You should include an aim, hypothesis, materials list, method, your results and how you will communicate your results.

FIGURE 4 A multimeter water tester

2 **Describe** what type of solution could be used as a control in this experiment and **justify** your answer.

1.4 Research investigation

In the Research investigation, you must evaluate a claim, by 'researching, analysing and interpreting secondary evidence from scientific texts' to justify a conclusion about the claim (see Figure 5).

In the Student experiment, you used primary evidence, that is, data from experiments that you carried out. In the Research investigation, you will use secondary evidence; this includes reports of findings and conclusions from other people, such as scientific articles published in journals. A review of original research articles will also be useful because they can provide an interpretation or summary of the current state of knowledge in a particular area. The authors of secondary evidence will have made judgements about what are the most important research findings to draw to the attention of their readers. Secondary evidence also includes textbooks and other specialist books in an area, as well as chemical encyclopedias.

The evidence used for this task must come from scientifically credible resources. These resources may be scientific journals, books written by experts in the area, websites of government bodies, such as the CSIRO (Commonwealth Scientific and Industrial Research Organisation) or technical information provided by chemical supplier companies or instrument manufacturers.

To start the task, you must:

- select a claim to be evaluated – this may require some background general research first. Your teacher will provide guidance when you are forming your claim.
- come up with a research strategy by identifying the relevant scientific concepts that connect with the claim. A lot of time could be lost by not having a plan for the research.

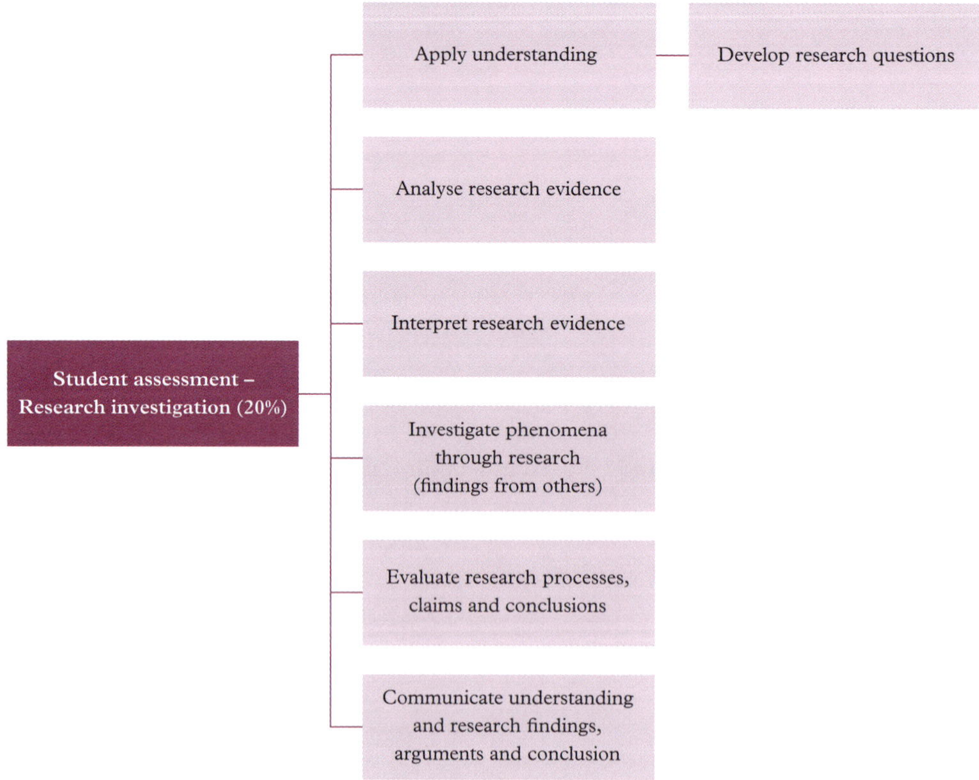

FIGURE 5 Key aspects of the Research investigation

RESEARCH REVIEW 1

Credible and non-credible resources

Some industries that benefit from molecular engineering processes include energy production and storage/conversion, agriculture, water treatment, disease diagnosis/screening, drug delivery systems, food processing/storage, air pollution/management, building and construction materials, health monitoring and pest detection or control.

1 **Investigate** one of the industries mentioned above and **identify** one credible resource and one non-credible resource on a molecular engineering process. **Summarise** why they were or were not credible below.

Resource 1

Source:

Why was it credible or not?

Resource 2

Source:

Why was it credible or not?

Equilibrium, acids and redox

PRACTICALS IN THIS UNIT

	SUGGESTED PRACTICAL	**2.2A** Effect of concentration on equilibrium
	SUGGESTED PRACTICAL	**2.2B** Effect of volume and pressure on equilibrium (TEACHER-ONLY DEMONSTRATION)
	SUGGESTED PRACTICAL	**2.2C** Effect of temperature on equilibrium (TEACHER-ONLY DEMONSTRATION)
	SUGGESTED PRACTICAL	**3.7** Measuring pH
	SUGGESTED PRACTICAL	**4.1** Electrical conductivity of strong and weak acids and bases
	MANDATORY PRACTICAL	**5.1A** Titration of hydrochloric acid with a standard sodium carbonate solution
	MANDATORY PRACTICAL	**5.1B** Determining the concentration of ethanoic acid in white vinegar
	MANDATORY PRACTICAL	**6.1** Performing single displacement reactions
	MANDATORY PRACTICAL	**7.1** Constructing a galvanic cell
	SUGGESTED PRACTICAL	**8.1A** Electrolysis of water
	SUGGESTED PRACTICAL	**8.1B** Electroplating of copper

WORD WIZARD

Draw a line to match each term with the correct definition.

ENTHALPY	the addition of a solution of known concentration to a known volume of another solution of unknown concentration until the reaction reaches neutralisation
DYNAMIC EQUILIBRIUM	the attraction between a positively charged nucleus and the negatively charged electrons of a neighbouring atom
MONOPROTIC ACID	the energy stored within chemical substances, referred to as its chemical energy or heat content
ELECTRICAL CONDUCTIVITY	the positively charged electrode, where reduction occurs
pK_a	an acid that can donate one hydrogen ion per molecule
STRONG BASE	an equation that represents either an oxidation or a reduction half of a chemical equation; it includes electrons to demonstrate electron transfer
END POINT	a galvanic cell that produces electricity by using a constant supply of reactants (often hydrogen and oxygen) and inert electrodes that do not break down
TITRATION	a reactant that causes another reactant to gain electrons and be reduced and is itself oxidised
OXIDATION	the point in a titration when the indicator changes colour
ELECTRONEGATIVITY	the state a reaction reaches when the rates of the forward and reverse reactions are equal
OXIDATION NUMBER	the degree to which a material conducts an electric current
HALF-EQUATION	a base that completely ionises in water
GALVANIC CELL	the process by which electrical energy is passed into a cell, using a power source, resulting in the reversal of spontaneous redox reactions
CATHODE	the number of electrons gained or lost by an atom
FUEL CELL	a measure of acid strength; the negative common logarithm (to base 10) of the acid dissociation constant
ELECTROLYSIS	a loss of electrons from one atom or species to another atom or species
REDUCING AGENT	an electrochemical cell in which the reduction and oxidation half-equations are separated and connected through a circuit to generate electricity

Equilibrium

Chemical equilibrium is a dynamic state, where the forward and backward reactions have not stopped but are occurring at the same rate. During dynamic equilibrium, the amount and concentration of chemical substances remain constant, the total pressure is constant, the temperature is constant, and the reaction is incomplete.

Equilibrium law, the mathematical relationship or concentration fraction between the reactants and products, applies only to systems at equilibrium. This relationship is called the equilibrium constant and is given the symbol K_c.

For a chemical reaction:

$$aA + bB \rightleftharpoons cC + dD$$

$$K_c = \frac{[C]^c[D]^d}{[A]^a[B]^b}$$

where A, B, C and D are substances in solution or as gases; [ ] is the concentration of the reactants and products in molarity (M); and *a*, *b*, *c* and *d* are the respective coefficients.

Le Châtelier's principle says that for any system at equilibrium, if reaction conditions are altered, the system will try to partially reverse this change.

Concepts of equilibrium can be applied to important reactions, including the production of favourable product yields in chemical manufacturing, balancing undesirable oxidation reactions in wine and other alcoholic beverage manufacturing, transportation of oxygen and carbon dioxide in biological systems, and balancing the nutrient cycles in the atmosphere and hydrosphere.

CHAPTER CHECKLIST

Read this checklist before you complete this chapter's activities, then return to it to check your understanding before your assessments.

Once you have completed this chapter, you can use the 'I can …' statements to assess and rate your understanding of the topics covered by ticking the appropriate box in the 'rating column'.

I can …	Confidently	Partially	Not really
… explain dynamic equilibrium.			
… understand Le Châtelier's principle and construct equilibrium graphs.			
… construct an equilibrium expression for an equation.			
… calculate the equilibrium constant for an equation.			

DATA DRILL 2

Interpreting equilibrium graphs

Students at a university outreach excursion used a UV/Vis spectrometer to study the equilibrium reaction of iron(III) ions reacting with thiocyanate ions to form iron(III)-thiocyanate ions. The data collected is shown in Figure 1 below, followed by the chemical equation.

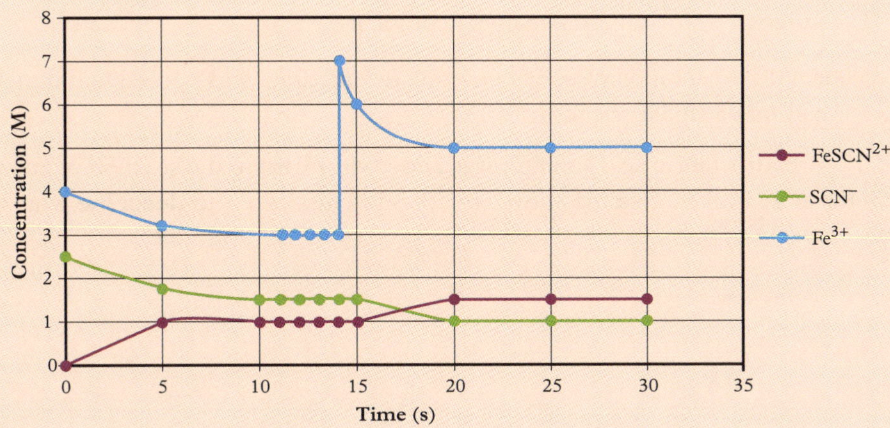

FIGURE 1 Iron(III) ions reacting with thiocyanate ions to form iron(III)-thiocyanate ions

$$Fe^{3+}(aq) + SCN^{-}(aq) \rightleftharpoons FeSCN^{2+}(aq)$$

1 **a** **Calculate** the approximate value of the equilibrium constant K_c from the concentrations at

i 10 seconds **ii** 20 seconds

b **Compare** and **consider** the difference between your calculated values from 1ai and 1aii above.

EXPERIMENT EXPLORER 2

Changing the equilibrium of a reaction

The cobalt ion equilibrium system is represented by the following equation:

$$Co(H_2O)_6^{2+}(aq) + 4Cl^-(aq) \rightleftharpoons CoCl_4^{2-}(aq) + 6H_2O(l) \qquad \Delta H = +50 \text{ kJ mol}^{-1}$$

pink — blue

hydrated cobalt(II) complex — chloro cobalt(II) complex

A student prepared a 0.2 M solution of cobalt chloride hexahydrate and poured half into a large beaker and the other half into a smaller beaker.

1 Concentrated 12 M hydrochloric acid solution was added dropwise to the solution of cobalt chloride hexahydrate in the large beaker. **Use** the above equation to **consider** and **describe** what the student would observe.

2 The 0.2 M solution of cobalt chloride hexahydrate in the smaller beaker was placed in a pneumatic trough with warm water. **Describe** what the student would observe next.

3 After the warm water treatment, the smaller beaker was placed in a pneumatic trough containing water and ice. **Describe** what the student would observe next.

Study tip

With the equilibrium disturbances due to Le Châtelier's principle, always remember that the position of the equilibrium and the value of the equilibrium constant K_c for a reaction is only affected by a change in temperature.

RESEARCH REVIEW 2

Referencing scientific papers

Referencing your supporting literature is an important process to get right for both your Student experiment and Research investigation. There are many different referencing styles, but some common rules need to be addressed when you cite your resources. See the guidelines based on the American Psychological Association (APA) style (6th edition) below.

In-text citations (references within sentences in your report):

Cite the authors' name(s), followed by the date.

- For one author, write (Curnow, 2019).
- For two authors, write (Curnow and Shaw, 2019).
- For three or more authors, write (Curnow et al., 2019) using the Latin abbreviation 'et al.' (which means 'and others').

Reference list (at the end of the report):

- Cite the authors' name(s), date, article title, journal, volume number, issue number and page range (see Figure 2 for the parts of a reference; note that the format style depends on the referencing style).

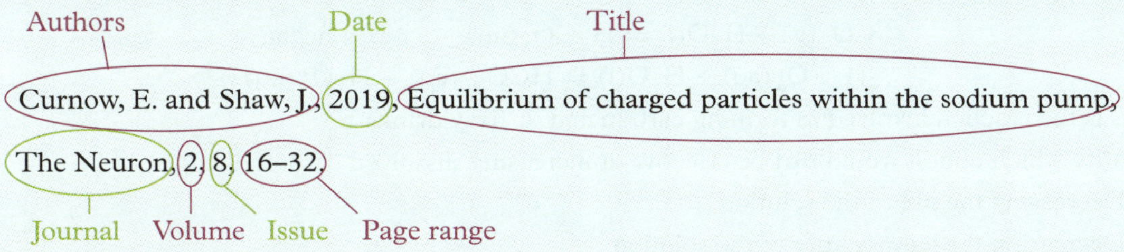

FIGURE 2 The parts of a reference in a reference list

1 **Identify** three different papers on Le Châtelier's principle and cite your references as they would appear both as in-text citations and as part of a reference list.

EXAM EXCELLENCE 2

Multiple choice – circle the correct answer

1 Identify the effect of adding a catalyst to a system at equilibrium:

A The value of E_a increases.

B The value of K_c increases.

C The net forward and reverse reaction rates increase.

D The concentration of products increases.

2 A sample of NOCl is allowed to come to equilibrium according to the following equation:

$$2NOCl(g) \rightleftharpoons 2NO(g) + Cl_2(g)$$

The volume of the mixture is halved and temperature remained constant. Identify what happens to the chlorine gas at the new equilibrium:

A Decreased in amount and decreased in concentration

B Increased in amount and decreased in concentration

C Decreased in amount and increased in concentration

D Increased in amount and increased in concentration.

3 Carbon dioxide gas dissolves to a small extent in water, forming carbonic acid in an exothermic reaction:

$$CO_2(g) + H_2O(l) \rightleftharpoons H_2CO_3(aq) \qquad \Delta H = \text{negative}$$
$$H_2CO_3(aq) + H_2O(l) \rightleftharpoons HCO_3^-(aq) + H_3O^+(aq)$$

This is the reaction involved in forming carbonated or fizzy drinks.

Identify which option would **not** be effective at increasing dissolved carbon dioxide:

A Decreasing the pH of the solution

B Decreasing the temperature of the solution

C Increasing the concentration of carbon dioxide in the gas

D Increasing the pressure of the carbon dioxide gas.

4 The solubility of precipitates can be increased by using competing equilibria. Silver ions readily form a white precipitate of silver chloride but form a soluble complex with ammonia:

$$AgCl(s) \rightleftharpoons Ag^+(aq) + Cl^-(aq) \qquad K_c = 1.6 \times 10 -10$$
$$AgCl(s) + 2NH_3(aq) \rightleftharpoons Ag(NH_3)_2^+(aq) + Cl^-(aq) \qquad K_c = 1.6 \times 10^7$$

Identify how best to increase the solubility of the silver chloride precipitate, AgCl(s):

A Add sodium chloride solution to the mixture

B Add ammonia solution to the mixture

C Add silver ions in the form of silver nitrate solution to the mixture

D Add H^+ ions to the mixture.

5 An experiment is carried out to investigate the effect of temperature on the following reaction:

$$N_2O_4(g) \rightleftharpoons 2NO_2(g) \qquad \Delta H = +57\,kJ\,mol^{-1}$$

Identify the result of the experiment if the temperature increases:

A The K_c value will remain the same, but equilibrium will be reached more quickly

B The K_c value will remain the same, but equilibrium will be reached more slowly

C The K_c value will increase

D The K_c value will decrease.

Short answer

6 The solubility of carbon dioxide in natural systems is affected by a number of competing equilibria:

Equation 1 $CO_2(g) + H_2O(l) \rightleftharpoons H_2CO_3(aq)$

Equation 2 $H_2CO_3(aq) + Ca(OH)_2(aq) \rightleftharpoons CaCO_3(s) + 2H_2O(l)$

Equation 3 $CaCO_3(s) + CO_2(g) + H_2O(l) \rightleftharpoons Ca^{2+}(aq) + 2HCO_3^-(aq)$

a **Identify** one of the sources of the increased concentration of carbon dioxide in the air over the past 200 years.

____

____

b **Use** the equation(s) above and your knowledge of Le Châtelier's principle to **consider** how the oceans can act as a carbon dioxide sink.

____

____

____

____

7 The equilibrium for the reaction of nitrogen dioxide to form nitrogen tetroxide is shown:

$$2NO_2(g) \rightleftharpoons N_2O_4(g) \quad K_c = 170 \text{ at } 298\text{ K}$$

A mixture of the gases was found to contain 0.015 M NO_2 gas and 0.025 M N_2O_4 gas.

a **Calculate** the reaction quotient (Q_c) for the mixture shown.

b **Deduce** whether the mixture shown is at equilibrium. If not, **identify** whether more N_2O_4 or NO_2 should be formed for the mixture to reach equilibrium.

____

____

____

8 **Consider** the following equilibrium system:

$$CO(g) + 2H_2(g) \rightleftharpoons CH_3OH(g) \qquad \Delta H = -90\text{ kJ mol}^{-1}$$

Use Table 1 on the following page, to **describe** what happens to the system after the following changes are made:

TABLE 1 Changes to and effects on the equilibrium system

Change to the system	Net shift	Effect on the number of moles of H_2
Addition of nitrogen		No effect
Decrease in pressure	Left	
Increase in temperature		Increase
Volume halved		
Methanol removed	Right	

9 The equation for the equilibrium system for the production of nitrogen trichloride is:

$$N_2(g) + 3Cl_2(g) \rightleftharpoons 2NCl_3(g) \qquad \Delta H = +223\,kJ\,mol^{-1}$$

Sketch the concentration vs time graphs for Cl_2 and NCl_3 on the graph below, incorporating the following changes:

- At 5 minutes, the temperature is increased.
- The system establishes equilibrium again.
- At 18 minutes, the concentration of Cl_2 is increased.
- The system re-establishes equilibrium again at 20 minutes.
- All concentrations are 1 M and the temperature of the reaction is 25°C. **Note:** The graph N_2(g) line has been provided for you.

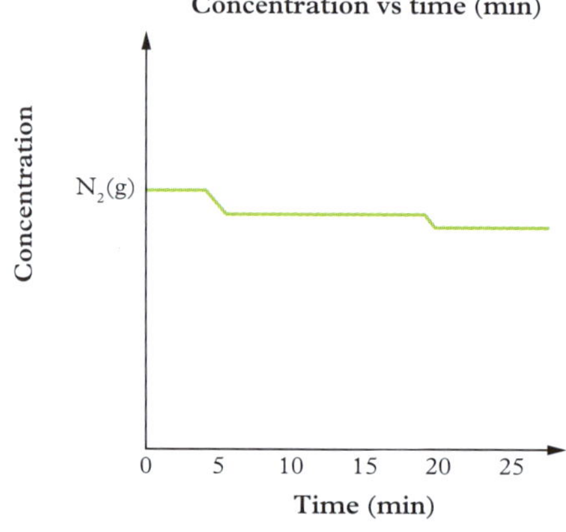

10 The equilibrium constant for a chemical reaction occurring at a fixed temperature with gaseous reactants and products can be expressed as:

$$K_c = \frac{[C][D]^3}{[A]^2[B]}$$
$$= 7.46 \times 10^5$$

a **Construct** the balanced chemical equation for the reaction involving gases A, B, C and D.

____

b **Deduce** the ratio of reactants to products when this reaction mixture is at equilibrium.

____

CHAPTER

Acids and bases

An acid is a proton donor according to the Bronsted-Lowry definition. Monoprotic acids can donate one proton per molecule (e.g. HCl). Diprotic acids can donate two protons (e.g. H_2SO_4), and triprotic acids can donate three protons (e.g. H_3PO_4). The first ionisation occurs to a greater extent than the second or third ionisation steps.

A base (e.g. NaOH) is a proton acceptor in terms of the Bronsted-Lowry definition, or has the ability to draw a proton away from an acid.

Amphiprotic substances (e.g. H_2O) can act as acids or bases, depending on the acidic or basic characteristics of the other reactant involved. Water can also self-ionise.

The pH scale is a way of expressing the strength of acids and bases and is a logarithmic scale.

$$pH = -\log_{10}[H^+]$$

The pOH scale is a way of expressing the concentration of hydroxide ions in solution.

$$pOH = -\log_{10}[OH^-]$$

When solving problems to find out the concentration of H^+ ions, use

$$[H^+] = 10^{-pH}.$$

Because acids and bases are opposites, pH and pOH are also opposites and

$$pH + pOH = 14.$$

A conjugate acid–base pair is formed when an acid reacts with a base.

$HCl(aq)$	+ $H_2O(l)$	→ $H_3O^+(aq)$	+ $Cl^-(aq)$
acid	base	conjugate acid of water	conjugate base of HCl

Le Châtelier's principle is used to predict how buffer solutions respond when acids or bases are added.

CHAPTER CHECKLIST

Read this checklist before you complete this chapter's activities, then return to it to check your understanding before your assessments.

Once you have completed this chapter, you can use the 'I can …' statements to assess and rate your understanding of the topics covered by ticking the appropriate box in the 'rating column'.

I can …	Confidently	Partially	Not really
… describe the properties of acids and bases.			
… understand the electrical conductivity properties of acids and bases.			
… calculate concentrations, pH and pOH.			
… explain the Brønsted–Lowry model.			

DATA DRILL 3

Acidification of the ocean – reading scientific datasets

The impact of CO_2 levels off the coast of Hawaii are shown in the graph below (Figure 1).

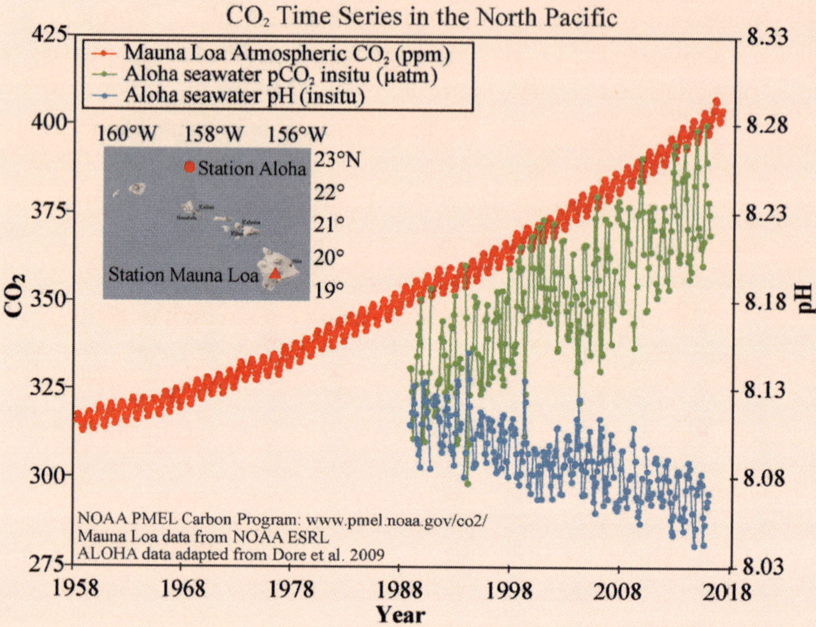

FIGURE 1 Impact of CO_2 levels off the coast of Hawaii

1 a **Identify** the relationship between the measured levels of CO_2 in the atmosphere and time. **Use** evidence from Figure 1 to support your answer.

b **Identify** the relationship between the measured levels of CO_2 in the seawater and time. **Use** evidence from Figure 1 to support your answer.

c **Use** your answers from 1a and 1b above to **identify** the relationship between the measured levels of CO_2 in the atmosphere (and in the seawater) and the pH of the seawater. **Use** evidence from Figure 1 to support your answer.

EXPERIMENT EXPLORER 3

Measuring the pH of household substances

1 **Describe** how you would **design** an experiment, using a calibrated digital pH meter (Figure 2), to measure the pH of household substances and **classify** them as acids, bases or neutral substances. You should include an aim, hypothesis, materials list, method, results and how you will communicate your results.

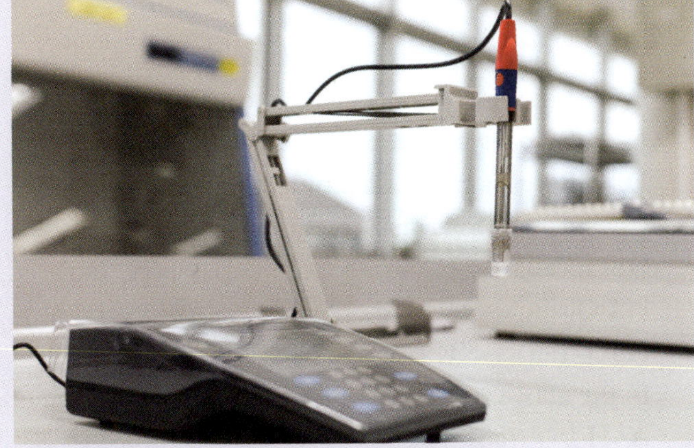

FIGURE 2 A calibrated digital pH meter

RESEARCH REVIEW 3

Credible and non-credible resources

1 **Based** on the hypothesis that you developed for 'Measuring the pH of household substances' in Experiment explorer 3, **use** the internet to **identify** one credible resource. **Summarise** why it is credible below.

Resource

Title:

Why is it credible?

EXAM EXCELLENCE 3

Multiple choice – circle the correct answer

1 For $HS^-(aq)$:

A $H_2S(aq)$ is the strong conjugate acid.

B $H_2S(aq)$ is the weak conjugate acid.

C $H_2S(aq)$ is the strong conjugate base.

D $H_2S(aq)$ is the weak conjugate base.

2 Consider the following reactions:

$HSO_4^-(aq) + NH_3(aq) \rightarrow SO_4^{2-}(aq) + NH_4^+(aq)$

$H_2PO_4^-(aq) + NH_3(aq) \rightarrow HPO_4^{2-}(aq) + NH_4^+(aq)$

$HSO_4^-(aq) + NH_4^+(aq) \rightarrow H_2SO_4(aq) + NH_3(aq)$

In the above reactions, which of the following is acting as an amphiprotic substance?

A $H_2PO_4^-(aq)$

B $NH_4^+(aq)$

C $NH_3(aq)$

D $HSO_4^-(aq)$

3 A 4.0 M solution of CH_3COOH is:

A a dilute strong acid

B a dilute weak acid

C a concentrated strong acid

D a concentrated weak acid.

4 Which of the following solutions is the most acidic?

A Hydrogen chloride in water, $[H^+] = 0.001$ M

B Potassium hydroxide in water, $[OH^-] = 10^{-5}$ M

C Ethanoic acid in water, $[H^+] = 0.00005$ M

D Sodium hydroxide in water, $[OH^-] = 0.001$ M

5 The pH of solution X is 8, and the pH of solution Y is 10. Which statement is correct about the hydrogen ion concentration, $[H^+]$, in the two solutions?

A The $[H^+]$ in X is 10 times more than that in Y.

B The $[H^+]$ in X is 100 times more than that in Y.

C The $[H^+]$ in X is 8 times more than that in Y.

D The $[H^+]$ in X is 0.1 times more than that in Y.

Short answer

6 **Construct** balanced chemical equations, including states, to show that in water:

a chromic acid (H_2CrO_4) is a diprotic acid.

____

b PH_3 is a weak base.

____

7 **a** The pH of a solution of HCl is 2.4. **Calculate** the concentration of H^+ ions.

b For a 2 M aqueous solution of NaOH, **calculate** the pH of the solution.

8 In aqueous solution, HBr dissociates completely, whereas HOI ionises partially.

a **Construct** balanced chemical equations showing these two situations.

b For each equation, **identify** the conjugate acid–base pairs.

9 A buffering agent for soil treatment can be manufactured by using a solution of dihydrogen phosphate, according to the following equilibrium equation:

$$H_2PO_4^-(aq) + H_2O(l) \rightleftharpoons HPO_4^{2-}(aq) + H_3O^+(aq) \quad pK_a \approx 7$$

Determine which species will be present in the soil at a higher concentration if this buffering agent is used in soil that is acidic.

10 Formic acid, with the formula HCOOH, is a weak monoprotic acid found in many insect stings and is partially responsible for the pain they cause. A particular formic acid solution has a pH of 4.0.

a **Determine** the hydrogen ion concentration of the formic acid solution.

b **Construct** an equation to show formic acid acting as a weak monoprotic acid in water.

CHAPTER 4 Dissociation constants and acid-base indicators

Acid or base strength is determined by the extent of their ionisation in solution, and it is represented by the dissociation constants K_a and K_b.

If K_a or K_b is large, then the right side of the ionisation equilibrium reaction is preferred. If K_a or K_b is smaller than 1, then the left side of the ionisation equilibrium reaction is preferred.

A strategy for the calculation of K_a (or K_b), by using the concentrations of reactants and products, is to construct and complete a RICE table.

Indicators are compounds that are often weak acids or bases, ionise to a small extent and have different colours in acidic or basic solutions.

When the equilibrium law is applied to the weak acid indicator equation,

$$K_a = [H^+] \text{ and } pK_a = pH$$

which signals the indicator colour change.

Indicators are used in colorimetric titrations, changing colour at (or very close to) the equivalence point, when neutralisation is complete. The indicator changes colour at the end point. By careful choice of indicator, the volumes for the end point and equivalence point are the same.

CHAPTER CHECKLIST

Read this checklist before you complete this chapter's activities, then return to it to check your understanding before your assessments.

Once you have completed this chapter, you can use the 'I can …' statements to assess and rate your understanding of the topics covered by ticking the appropriate box in the 'rating column'.

I can …	Confidently	Partially	Not really
… construct chemical equations and equilibrium constants for acids and bases.			
… calculate dissociation constants and concentrations.			
… understand the relationship between pK_a and pH.			
… recognise the strengths of acids and bases through titration curves.			

DATA DRILL 4

Organic acid pK_a values and extrapolating data

The pK_a values at 25°C for a series of organic acids is shown in Table 1 below. **Note:** The pK_a of acids is not effected by molar mass.

TABLE 1 pK_a values at 25°C for a homologous series of organic acids

Acid	Condensed formula	Molar mass	pK_a
Formic acid	HCOOH		3.75
Acetic acid	CH_3COOH		4.76
Propanoic acid	CH_3CH_2COOH		4.87
Butanoic acid	$CH_3(CH_2)_2COOH$		4.83
Pentanoic acid	$CH_3(CH_2)_3COOH$		4.83
Hexanoic acid	$CH_3(CH_2)_4COOH$		4.85
Heptanoic acid	$CH_3(CH_2)_5COOH$		4.89
Octanoic acid	$CH_3(CH_2)_6COOH$		4.89
Nonanoic acid	$CH_3(CH_2)_7COOH$		4.96

1 a **Calculate** the molar mass of each organic acid and record the data in Table 1.

b **Construct** a graph of the data in Table 1 and **identify** the relationship between molar mass and pK_a.

c **Extrapolate** the data in your graph to **predict** the pK_a of decanoic acid ($CH_3(CH_2)_8COOH$).

EXPERIMENT EXPLORER 4

Determining an indicator for a titration

The following indicators in Table 2 are offered to a class for their titration experiment.

TABLE 2 Indicators available for the titration experiment

Indicator	pH range	Colour
Alizarin red S	4.0–5.6	Red to yellow
Azolitmin	4.5–8.3	Red to blue
Bromophenol blue	3.0–4.6	Yellow to blue
Bromocresol green	4.0–5.6	Yellow to blue
Cresol red	7.2–8.8	Yellow to red
Cresolphthalein (meta)	1.2–2.8	Red to yellow (first change)
Cresolphthalein (meta)	7.4–9.0	Yellow to purple (second change)
Cresolphthalein (ortho)	8.2–9.8	Colourless to violet/red
Methyl red	4.2–6.2	Pink to yellow
Phenol red	6.8–8.2	Yellow to red

1 **Decide** which indicator(s) would be suitable for the following titration curves.

a

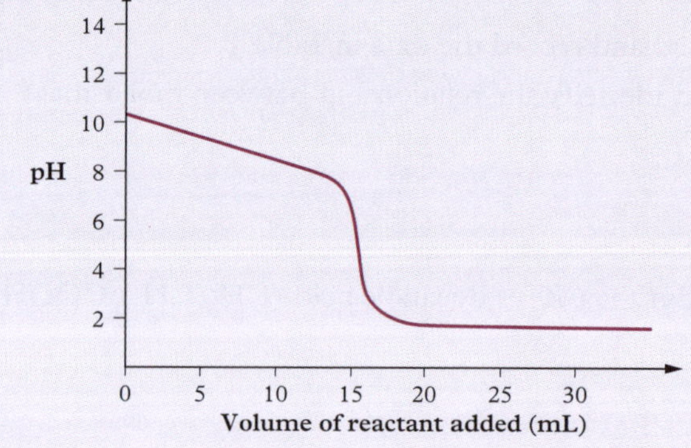

b

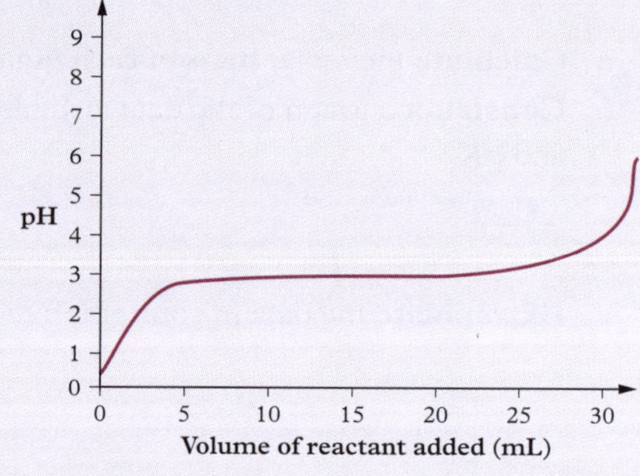

______________________ ______________________

RESEARCH REVIEW 4

Writing a research question

The following claim was suggested about superacids:

Superacids are substantially stronger than sulfuric acid and can be used to break down oil.

1 **Create** a research question(s) for this claim.

____

____

____

____

EXAM EXCELLENCE 4

Multiple choice - circle the correct answer

1 Boric acid (H_3BO_3) is often used as an eyewash to treat eye infections. A 0.050 M solution of boric acid has a pH of 5.28. The ionisation constant (K_a) of boric acid is:

A 5.25×10^{-6}

B 5.51×10^{-10}

C 5.43×10^{-8}

D 5.79×10^{-4}

2 The pH of a 0.500 M solution of trimethylamine, with a formula of $(CH_3)_3N$ and $pK_b = 4.13$, is:

A 2.22

B 11.8

C 4.42

D 5.91

3 How would you calculate K_b for the formate ion, given that $K_a = 1.8 \times 10^{-4}$ for formic acid?

A $K_b = K_a \times K_w$

B $K_b = \frac{K_w}{K_a}$

C $K_b = \frac{K_a}{K_w}$

D $K_b = K_w + K_a$

4 Use the following acid ionisation constants to solve for the correct base strength in decreasing order (i.e. strongest base first and weakest base last).

HF: $K_a = 7.2 \times 10^{-4}$; HNO_2: $K_a = 4.5 \times 10^{-4}$; HCN: $K_a = 6.2 \times 10^{-10}$

A $CN^- > NO_2^- > F^-$

B $NO_2^- > F^- > CN^-$

C $F^- > CN^- > NO_2^-$

D $F^- > NO_2^- > CN^-$

5 What is the equilibrium constant expression for the equilibrium in an aqueous solution of $NaHSO_3$?

A $\frac{[H_3O^+][SO_3^{2-}]}{[HSO_3^-]}$

B $\frac{[OH^-][H_2SO_3]}{[HSO_3^-]}$

C $\frac{[HSO_3^-]}{[H_3O^+][SO_3^{2-}]}$

D $\frac{[HSO_3^-]}{[OH^-][H_2SO_3]}$

Short answer

6 Hypochlorous acid (HOCl) is a weak monoprotic acid with a $K_a = 3.5 \times 10^{-8}$ at 25°C.

a **Construct** the equation for the hydrolysis (ionisation) of hypochlorous acid.

____

b **Calculate** the pH of a 0.5 M solution of hypochlorous acid.

c **Calculate** the percentage ionisation of hypochlorous acid.

7 A weak organic base aniline ($C_6H_5NH_2$) has a $K_b = 4.3 \times 10^{-10}$. **Calculate** the initial concentration of an aniline solution that has a pH of 8.8.

8 At 25°C, a 1.0 M solution of hydrogen sulfide (H_2S) has a pH of 3.75. **Calculate** the value of K_a at this temperature. **Note:** only one proton dissociates here.

9 A chemical indicator HIn^- is yellow in colour but turns red in the presence of acid. **Construct** the equilibrium equation that represents this colour change and **identify** the chemical species involved.

10 **Calculate** $[H_3O^+]$ of a solution of 0.1 M nitrous acid ($HNO_2(aq)$) with a $K_a = 4 \times 10^{-4}$.

Volumetric analysis

Volumetric analysis is an analytical technique that determines the unknown concentration of a solution by titrating it against a solution of known concentration.

The process involves:

- making a standard solution, with an accurately known concentration and volume from a (dry) primary standard in a volumetric flask. This standard solution is poured carefully into the burette.
- measuring accurately a specific volume of a solution of unknown concentration (called an aliquot) with an analytical pipette, which is drained into a conical flask.
- using a burette to deliver accurately known but variable volumes of the standard solution (called a titre). The volume is always read at the bottom of the meniscus for aqueous solutions.

The standard solution is slowly added (titrated) to the solution of unknown concentration in the conical flask (analyte/titrand) until they reach stoichiometrically equivalent amounts (i.e. the mole ratio has been reached). This is called the equivalence point.

An indicator is added to the titrand and changes colour at (or very close to) the equivalence point of the titration. The point at which the indicator changes colour is the end point.

Titrations are performed so that titres are close together, or differ by a maximum of 0.10 mL from highest to lowest. These are concordant results and are averaged to determine the mean titre.

In acid–base titrations, stoichiometry is used to find the relative amounts of acid or base required for neutralisation. When weak acids or bases are titrated against strong bases or acids respectively, a buffer region occurs. The midpoint (pK_a or pK_b) of this region, where the titre concentration is half the analyte's original concentration, is used to determine the concentration of the weak acid or base.

CHAPTER CHECKLIST

Read this checklist before you complete this chapter's activities, then return to it to check your understanding before your assessments.

Once you have completed this chapter, you can use the 'I can …' statements to assess and rate your understanding of the topics covered by ticking the appropriate box in the 'rating column'.

I can …	Confidently	Partially	Not really
… perform a titration.			
… understand titration curves.			
… identify the equivalence point.			
… understand the relationship between pK_a and K_a.			

DATA DRILL 5

Titration curves

A student used a pH meter to produce a titration curve and recorded their results in Figure 1.

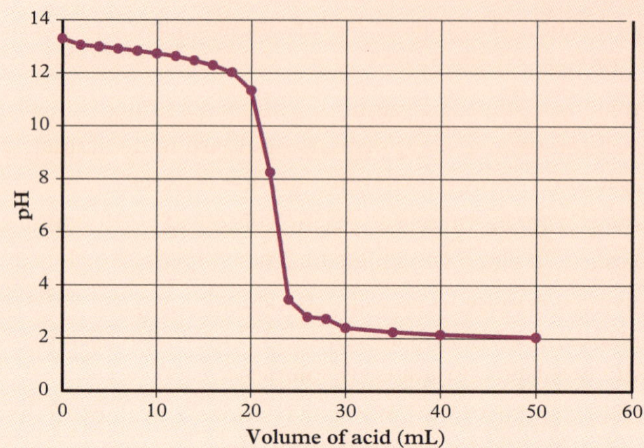

FIGURE 1 Titration curve

1 **Use** the graph to **identify** what types of acid and base are present. **Identify** the end point and the equivalence point on the titration curve. **Identify** the volume of titrant required to reach the equivalence point.

2 **Determine** a suitable indicator for this titration and **justify** your answer.

EXPERIMENT EXPLORER 5

Writing a risk assessment for a volumetric analysis experiment

A student has the following equipment and reagent list to perform a titration experiment:

- Glass pipette with pipette filler
- Conical flask
- Burette
- White tile
- Small glass funnel
- Retort stand with boss head and clamp
- Phenolphthalein indicator
- Solution of acid
- Solution of base

Use Table 1 to **create** a risk assessment for this experiment. Remember to include the hazards and risks of the products formed in this experiment.

TABLE 1 Hazards and risks of the experiment

Hazard	What are the risks?	What is the level of risk? (high/medium/low)	What are the controls?

RESEARCH REVIEW 5

Designing a poster

Industrial applications of titrations are found in the pharmaceutical, food, wine, environmental, biodiesel, and waste oil and waste water treatment industries.

1 **Select** one of the industries mentioned above and **create** a plan for a scientific poster that you can present to the class.

There are a few guidelines to follow when creating a poster, including:

- Bullet points are better than paragraphs of text.
- Pictures and diagrams are a great way to describe a process.
- People read from left to right and top to bottom. Try to lay out the poster in this way.
- A summary at the end of the poster gives clarity.
- Remember to include a title and key formulas, and don't overuse colour (three to four contrasting colours work well).

EXAM EXCELLENCE 5

Multiple choice – circle the correct answer

1 A student is titrating aliquots of phosphoric acid with potassium hydroxide solution. Which of the following would lead to an error in the results?

A Rinsing the pipette with the phosphoric acid solution

B Rinsing the three conical flasks with the phosphoric acid solution

C Having some water in the conical flasks before the aliquots are added

D Rinsing the burette with the potassium hydroxide solution.

2 Which of the following items is **not** used when preparing a standard solution of the primary standard potassium hydrogen phthalate for use in a volumetric analysis?

A Volumetric flask

B Hotplate

C Deionised water

D Electronic balance

3 What is the concentration of a sodium hydroxide solution if a 20.00 mL aliquot was titrated against a 0.05 M sulfuric acid solution, and the average titre was found to be 17.5 mL?

A 0.009 mol L^{-1}

B 0.04 mol L^{-1}

C 8.0 mol L^{-1}

D 0.09

4 Which of the following diagrams describes the relationship between the pH of a buffer solution and the volume of sodium hydroxide (NaOH) added to the solution?

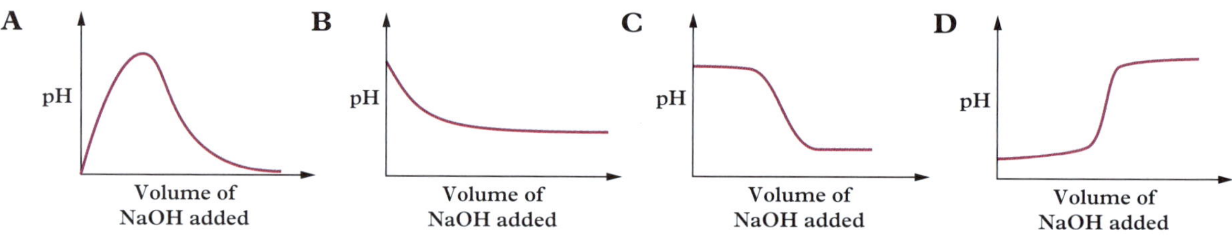

5 Oxalic acid dihydrate is a pure, stable crystalline substance. Which of the following best describes its use in an acid–base titration?

A Buffer

B Primary standard

C Chemical indicator

D Stoichiometric indicator

Short answer

6 An auto-electrician wants to test the concentration of battery acid (H_2SO_4).

- They dilute 25 mL of the concentrated battery acid to 250 mL in a volumetric flask, which is a dilution factor of 10.
- They fill a burette with this diluted acid.
- They titrate this acid against 20 mL aliquots of 0.203 M potassium hydroxide (KOH) solution, using phenolphthalein as the indicator.
- They identify end points of 10.82, 10.01, 9.95 and 10.03 mL.

a **Construct** the balanced chemical equation for this reaction, including the states.

____

b **Determine** the average titre.

____

c **Calculate** how many moles of KOH are in each aliquot.

d **Calculate** how many moles of H_2SO_4 react with each aliquot.

7 A titration was performed by the addition of a 0.175 M oxalic acid ($H_2C_2O_4$) solution to 25.00 mL aliquots of a sodium hydroxide (NaOH) solution. The data in Table 2 was collected.

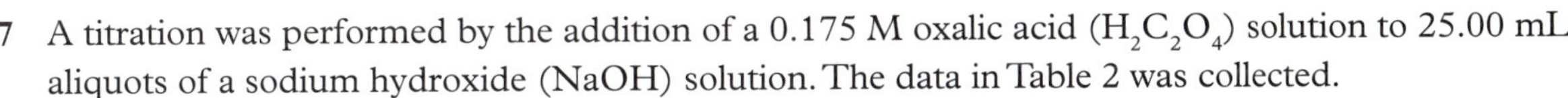

a **Construct** a balanced chemical equation for the reaction, including the states.

____

b **Calculate** the concentration of the sodium hydroxide solution.

TABLE 2 Results of the titration of oxalic acid with sodium hydroxide

	Trial 1	Trial 2	Trial 3
Final volume of $H_2C_2O_4$ (mL)	23.00	39.05	20.95
Initial volume of $H_2C_2O_4$ (mL)	4.85	23.00	5.00

8 A 0.1 M solution of an unknown acid was titrated with a 0.1 M sodium hydroxide solution, which resulted in the following titration curve (Figure 2).

a **Determine** a suitable indicator (which is not phenolphthalein) for this titration and **justify** your answer.

____

____

____

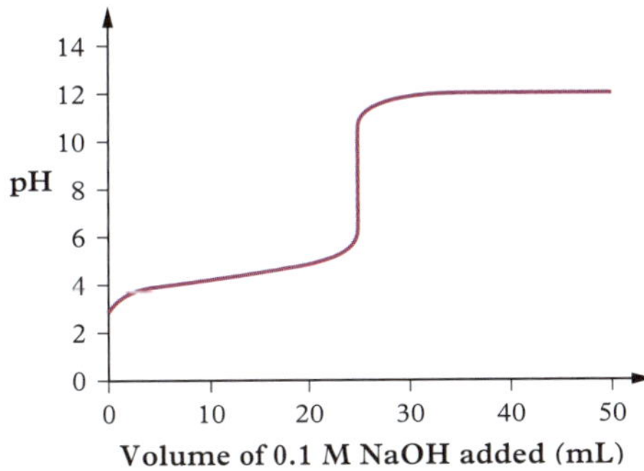

FIGURE 2 Titration curve of an unknown acid titrated with sodium hydroxide.

b **Deduce** whether the unknown acid is weak or strong and **justify** your answer.

____

____

____

____

9 A student conducted the following titration experiments:

- Titration A — A strong acid was titrated with a strong base.
- Titration B — A weak acid was titrated with a strong base.

a **Contrast** the two different pH at the equivalence points of Titration A and Titration B.

____

____

b **Explain** your answer for 9a above, using an equation(s) if necessary.

____

____

10 A chemistry class carried out a titration of aliquots of Windex™, using a 20 mL pipette, against a 0.102 M solution of hydrochloric acid. Phenolphthalein was the indicator.

The following titres of hydrochloric acid were obtained by two students: 22.37, 21.21, 21.28, 21.25 and 21.19 mL.

a **Construct** the balanced chemical equation for the reaction, including the states.

____

b **Determine** the average titre.

____

c **Calculate** how many moles of hydrochloric acid are in the average titre.

d **Calculate** how many moles of ammonia are in each aliquot of Windex™.

e **Determine** the concentration (molarity) of ammonia in the Windex™.

Redox reactions

Redox is an abbreviation for reduction and oxidation reactions, which occur together. This means that when an oxidation reaction occurs, a reduction reaction occurs at the same time.

Oxidation is the loss of electrons (OIL) from the valence shell of the reductant (an electron donor). Reduction is the gain of electrons (RIG) from the valence shell of the oxidant (an electron acceptor).

Assigning oxidation numbers to atoms in a reaction determines whether an oxidation or reduction reaction has occurred. Oxidation numbers of transition metal elements are written in roman numerals in brackets after the element's name, such as copper(II), or are written after the symbol, such as Cu^{2+} or Cu^{II}.

A decrease in oxidation number of an atom = reduction

An increase in oxidation number of an atom = oxidation

Half-equations represent either the oxidation part or the reduction part of a redox reaction; they show electrons being gained or lost, do not include spectator ions, and are combined to form overall redox reactions, as shown by the below examples:

Oxidation half-equation: $Zn(s) \rightarrow Zn^{2+}(aq) + 2e^-$

Reduction half-equation: $Ag^+(aq) + e^- \rightarrow Ag(s)$

Overall redox reaction: $Zn(s) + 2Ag^+(aq) \rightarrow Zn^{2+}(aq) + 2Ag(s)$

CHAPTER CHECKLIST

Read this checklist before you complete this chapter's activities, then return to it to check your understanding before your assessments.

Once you have completed this chapter, you can use the 'I can …' statements to assess and rate your understanding of the topics covered by ticking the appropriate box in the 'rating column'.

I can …	Confidently	Partially	Not really
… understand the transfer of electrons during oxidation and reduction.			
… understand redox reactions.			
… determine oxidation numbers.			
… construct and combine half-equations into overall redox equations.			

DATA DRILL 6

Reading graphs and extrapolating data

The graph in Figure 1 shows the blood alcohol concentration (BAC) per number of drinks for an Australian male with an average mass of 86 kg (in 2011–2012).

1 a **Define** and **calculate** the gradient between the BAC and the number of drinks for an Australian male. **Determine** the equation of the graph.

____

____

____

____

b Using the graph and your answer from 1a above, **predict** the BAC for an Australian male after 10 drinks, drawing on the graph.

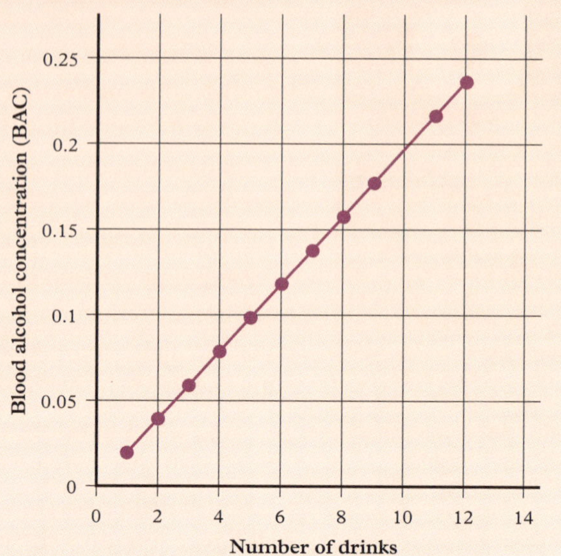

FIGURE 1 BAC per number of drinks for an Australian male with an average mass of 86 kg (in 2011–2012)

____

EXPERIMENT EXPLORER 6

Changing experimental conditions – metals in salt solution

1 Four strips of magnesium metal are added to four separate beakers containing solutions of the following metal salts: magnesium nitrate, zinc nitrate, copper(II) nitrate and silver(I) nitrate (Figure 2).

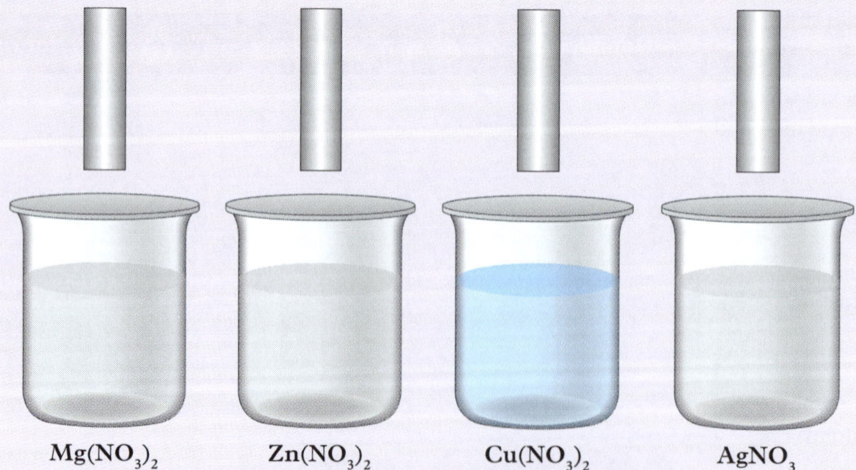

FIGURE 2 Magnesium metal is added to beakers containing solutions of different metal salts.

a In which beaker(s) would you **predict** a reaction will occur? **Describe** what you would expect to observe.

b **Construct** the half-equations for the beaker(s) in which you would observe a reaction. **Identify** which half-equations are oxidation and reduction reactions.

c What would you **predict** to observe in this experiment if you changed the metal strips from magnesium to copper metal? **Use** half-equations to support your answer.

Study tip

You may want to refer to a metal reactivity series to help answer the questions in Experiment explorer 6.

RESEARCH REVIEW 6

Writing a research question

The following claim was suggested about the manufacturing of steel:

Steel can only be produced from one type of iron ore in a blast furnace.

1 **Create** a research question(s) for this claim.

EXAM EXCELLENCE 6

Multiple choice – circle the correct answer

1 An equation for the reaction that may occur during the extraction of iron from iron ore is as follows:

$$Fe_2O_3(s) + 3CO(g) \rightarrow 2Fe(l) + 3CO_2(g)$$

During this reaction, the oxidation number of iron changes from:

A +3 to 0 and CO is the reductant.

B +6 to 0 and CO is the reductant.

C +3 to 0 and CO is the oxidant.

D +6 to 0 and CO is the oxidant.

2 Which of the following equations is a redox reaction?

A $H_2S(g) + 2OH^-(aq) \rightarrow S^{2-}(aq) + 2H_2O(l)$

B $SO_4^{2-}(aq) + H_3O^+(aq) \rightarrow HSO_4^-(aq) + H_2O(l)$

C $NH_4^+(aq) + CO_3^{2-}(aq) \rightarrow NH_3(g) + HCO_3^-(aq)$

D $I_2(aq) + 2OH^-(aq) \rightarrow I^-(aq) + IO^-(aq) + H_2O(l)$

3 The transition metal vanadium can exist in several oxidation states. The oxidation numbers for two vanadium species VO^{2+} and VO_4^{3-} are:

A +4 and +5

B +4 and +8

C +6 and +5

D +6 and +8

4 In the below reaction:

$$MnO_2(s) + 4HCl(aq) \rightarrow Cl_2(g) + 2H_2O(l) + MnCl_2(aq)$$

which of the following atom(s) have an oxidation number that changes?

A Mn

B Mn and Cl

C Mn, Cl and O

D Mn, Cl, O and H

5 In the following compounds – $H_2S_2O_7$, N_2O_5, HIO_3 and Cl_2O_7 – the atom with the highest oxidation number is:

A I

B S

C Cl

D N

Short answer

6 **Identify** the oxidation number of sulfur in the following substances: S, SO_2, SO_3, SO_4^{2-} and H_2S.

7 Two metals, A and B, are being investigated.

A rod of metal A is placed in a solution containing B^+ ions. A rod of metal B is placed in a solution containing A^+ ions, as per the following diagram in Figure 3.

No reaction occurs in Beaker 1. In Beaker 2, metal B slowly corrodes and becomes coated with metal A.

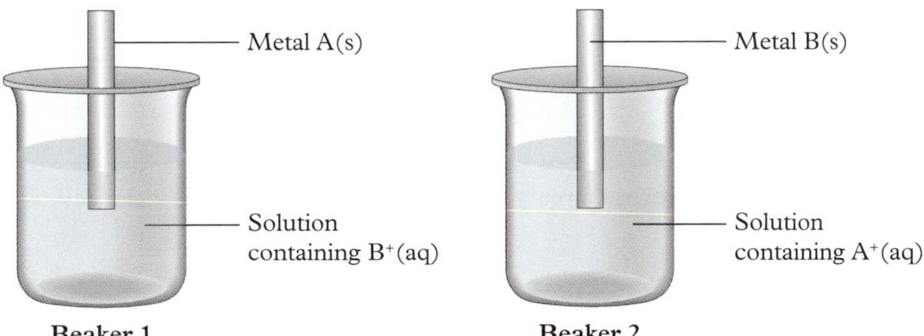

FIGURE 3 Investigation of the reactivity of two metals, A and B

a **Determine** which metal (A or B) is more reactive. **Explain** your answer.

b **Determine** which chemical (A, B, A^+ or B^+) is the strongest oxidant. **Explain** your answer using an equation(s).

8 For the following reaction:

$$Cr_2O_7^{2-}(aq) + 6H^+(aq) + 2NO(g) \rightarrow 2Cr^{3+}(aq) + 3H_2O(l) + 2NO_3^-(aq)$$

a **Define** the oxidant and the reductant.

b **Construct** the two balanced half-equations of this reaction. (**Hint:** The oxidation half-equation needs to be multiplied before combining with the reduction half-equation.)

9 **Determine** how you would **define** a reaction as a 'redox' reaction. **Use** balanced equations to **explain** your answer.

10 **Classify** which of the following reactions are redox reactions. Rewrite each equation with the oxidation numbers of the individual elements. If the reactions are redox reactions, **identify** the oxidant and the reductant.

a $2Na(s) + Cl_2(g) \rightarrow 2NaCl(s)$

b $Ca(OH)_2(aq) + 2HNO_3(aq) \rightarrow Ca(NO_3)_2(aq) + 2H_2O(l)$

c $AgNO_3(aq) + NaCl(aq) \rightarrow AgCl(s) + NaNO_3(aq)$

d $CuSO_4(aq) + Zn(s) \rightarrow Cu(s) + ZnSO_4(aq)$

Electrochemical cells and electrode potential

In galvanic cells, spontaneous chemical reactions convert chemical energy into electrical energy. The oxidation and reduction reactions are separated, and electrons travel by a wire (i.e. an external circuit) between the half-cells.

A galvanic cell contains two half-cells: one where oxidation occurs (the anode) and one where reduction occurs (the cathode).

Each half-cell contains:

- an electrode, conducting electrons in or out of the half-cell
- an electrolyte, containing ions moving freely through the solution.

The oxidation half-cell produces electrons and has a negative polarity.

The reduction half-cell consumes electrons and has a positive polarity.

The two half-cell reactions are producing or consuming ions in the electrolyte, unbalancing the total charge. To prevent this unbalance (and complete the circuit), the two half-cells are connected by a salt bridge, containing a source of mobile ions that flow between the half-cells and balance the electrolyte charges.

Reaction spontaneity and voltage generated by galvanic cells (i.e. the electromotive force, EMF) can be calculated using electrode potentials ($E°$) from the electrochemical series. Galvanic cells are used in non-rechargeable (primary) batteries, such as alkaline or button cell types. Fuel cells are another type of galvanic cell, producing electricity from the reagents of hydrogen (H_2) and oxygen (O_2) gas.

CHAPTER CHECKLIST

Read this checklist before you complete this chapter's activities, then return to it to check your understanding before your assessments.

Once you have completed this chapter, you can use the 'I can …' statements to assess and rate your understanding of the topics covered by ticking the appropriate box in the 'rating column'.

I can …	Confidently	Partially	Not really
… predict reaction occurrences with the electrochemical series.			
… explain how electricity is generated from redox reactions.			
… calculate voltages from redox reactions.			
… understand redox reactions in batteries and fuel cells.			

DATA DRILL 7

Electrochemical cells

A student set up an electrochemical cell (Figure 1) to investigate the effect of temperature on the measured cell voltage. The student used 1.0 M solutions of the electrolytes in the experiment. The results of the experiment are given in Table 1 below.

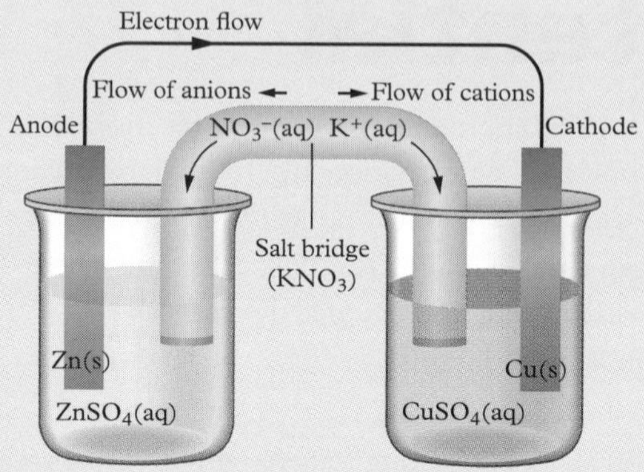

FIGURE 1 Electrochemical cell set-up for the temperature–voltage experiment

TABLE 1 Raw data recorded for the temperature–voltage experiment

Temperature (°C)	Trial 1 voltage (V)	Trial 2 voltage (V)	Trial 3 voltage (V)	Trial 4 voltage (V)	Trial 5 voltage (V)	Average voltage (V)
0	0.91	0.90	0.91	0.87	0.89	
3	0.91	0.94	0.90	0.95	0.93	
15	0.83	0.85	0.86	0.83	0.86	
22	0.84	0.85	0.82	0.86	0.85	
54	0.85	0.82	0.78	0.85	0.84	

1 a **Construct** the oxidation and reduction equations for the reactions occurring in the two half-cells.

b **Calculate** the average voltage reading for each temperature and record the data in Table 1.

c **Construct** a graph of average voltage vs temperature and **identify** the relationship.

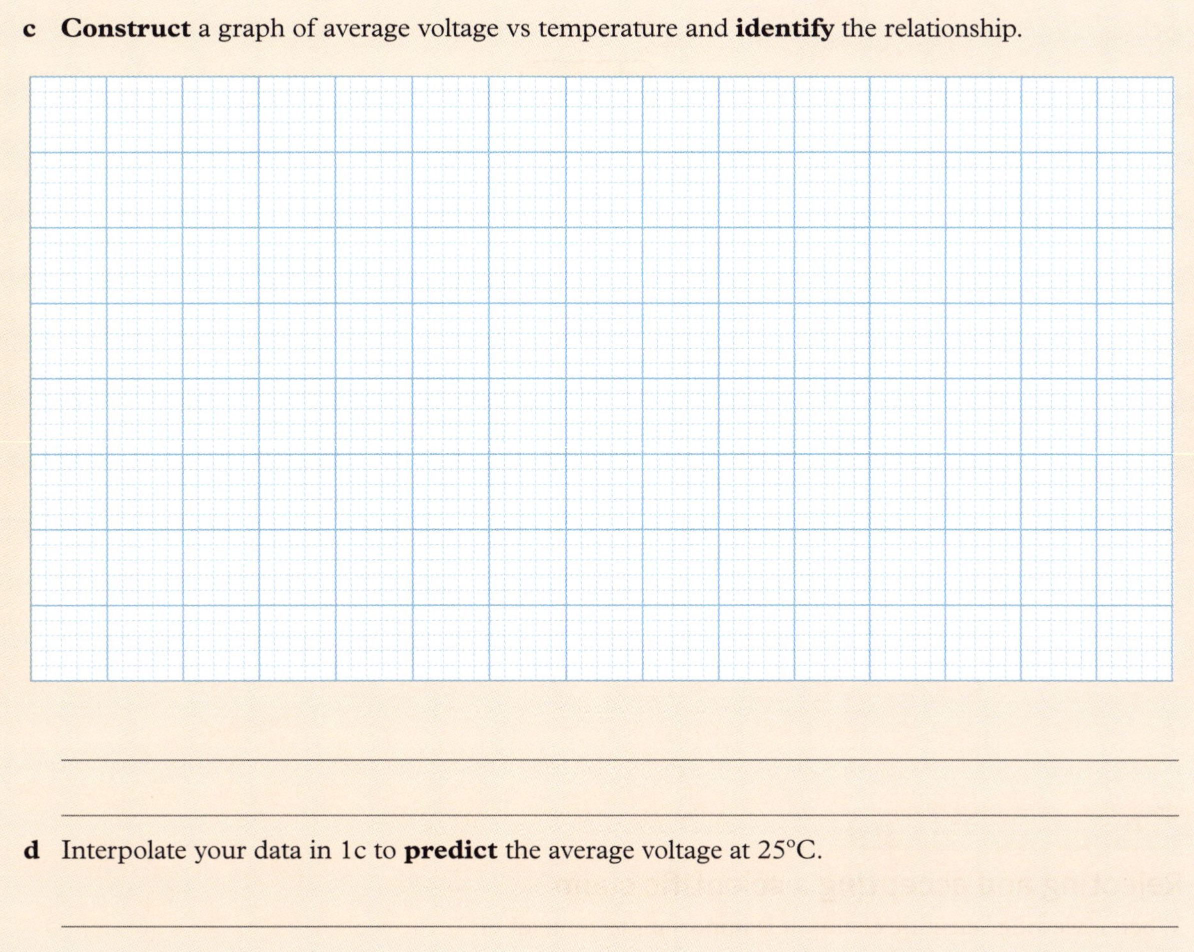

____

____

d Interpolate your data in 1c to **predict** the average voltage at 25°C.

____

EXPERIMENT EXPLORER 7

Constructing galvanic cells

A class was divided into groups to construct a galvanic cell using the materials in Table 2.

1 **Use** Figure 2 on the next page to **identify**:
- the anode and polarity (positive or negative)
- the cathode and polarity
- the flow of electrons
- the movement of salt bridge anions and cations
- the material of the electrodes
- the electrolyte solutions
- the half-cell equations
- the overall cell equation
- the theoretical voltage generated using E° values from the electrochemical series.

TABLE 2 Materials used in the galvanic cell

Galvanic cell
Copper metal
Graphite rod (carbon)
Silver nitrate solution
Copper nitrate solution
Potassium nitrate solution
Voltmeter
Filter paper (folded)
Connecting wires/clips
Beakers

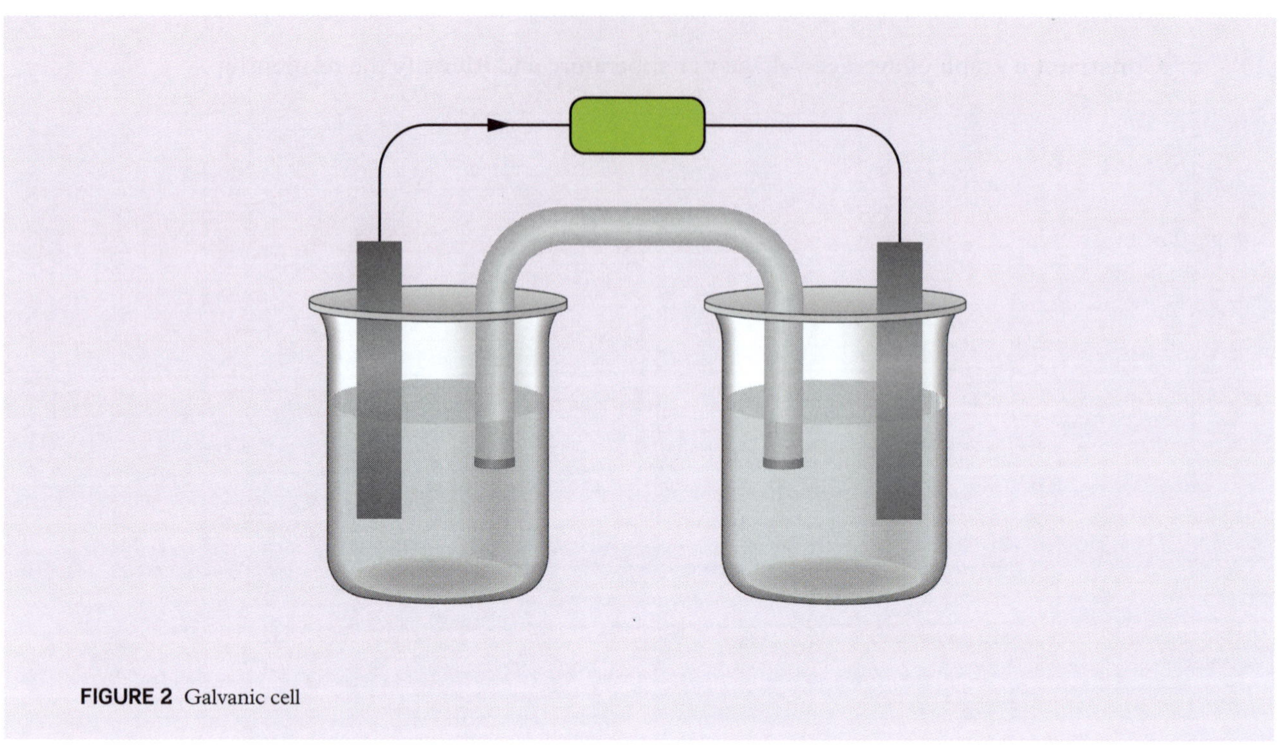

FIGURE 2 Galvanic cell

RESEARCH REVIEW 7

Rejecting and accepting a scientific claim

When reviewing scientific claims, it is important to remember:

- What is the source of the claim? Is it trustworthy?
- Does the claim make sense or is it incorrect?
- Is it based on credible data? Are there scientific measurements?
- Are the scientific 'facts' widely accepted in the scientific community?

1 **Investigate** the following two claims about fuel cells and **identify** which one is more credible and why.

There is only one type of fuel cell available in the marketplace with limited usage.

Fuel cells are an integral part of space travel.

2 **Create** a research question(s) for the credible claim.

EXAM EXCELLENCE 7

Multiple choice – circle the correct answer

The information in Figure 3 refers to Questions 1 and 2.

1 As the cell operates, electrons flow to:

A the lead (Pb) electrode, where lead is oxidised.

B the cadmium (Cd) electrode, where cadmium is oxidised.

C the lead electrode, where Pb^{2+} is reduced.

D the cadmium electrode, where Cd^{2+} is reduced.

2 The E° value for the cell is:

A –0.4 V

B +0.27 V

C +0.14 V

D +0.40 V

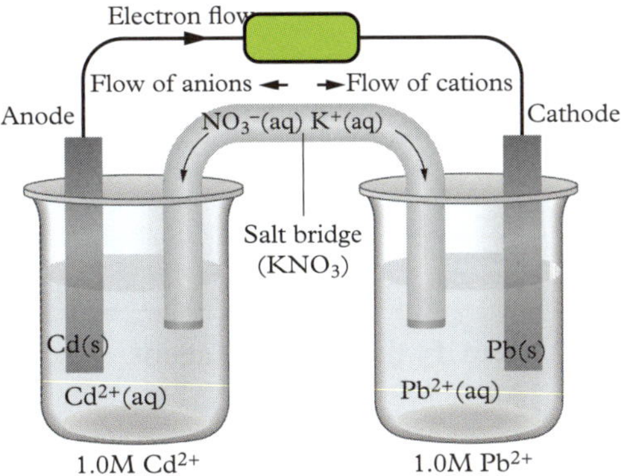

FIGURE 3 Electrochemical cell with lead and cadmium

3 For the electrochemical cell in Figure 4, the initial voltage of the cell would be:

A +0.48 V

B –0.48 V

C 0.00 V

D +1.04 V

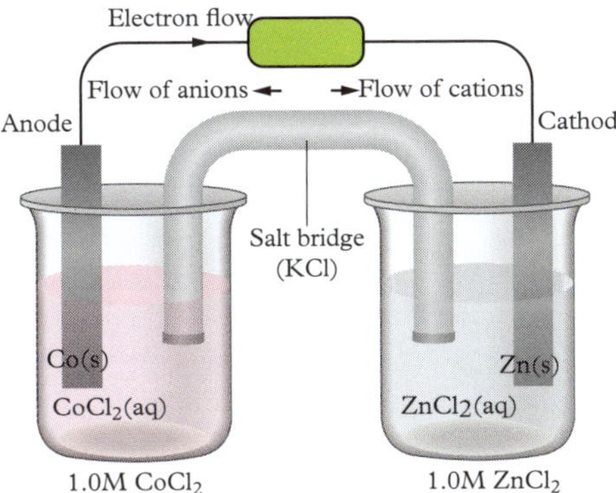

FIGURE 4 Electrochemical cell with cobalt and zinc

4 The salt bridge in a galvanic cell:

A completes the circuit by allowing electrons to flow between the half-cells.

B completes the circuit by allowing electrons to flow from the cathode to the anode.

C provides anions and cations to react at the electrodes in each half-cell.

D provides anions and cations to maintain charge balance in each half-cell.

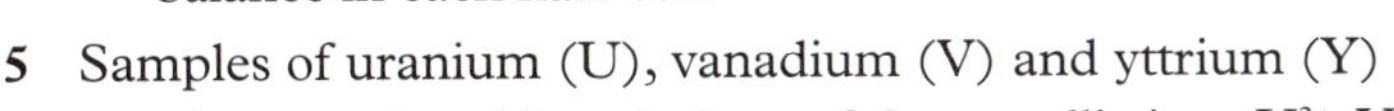

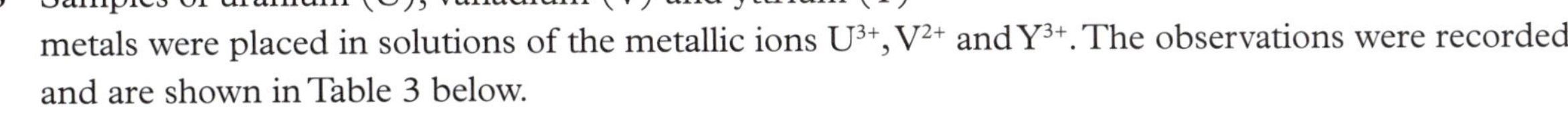

5 Samples of uranium (U), vanadium (V) and yttrium (Y) metals were placed in solutions of the metallic ions U^{3+}, V^{2+} and Y^{3+}. The observations were recorded and are shown in Table 3 below.

The order of oxidising agents from the strongest to the weakest are:

A V^{2+}, U^{3+}, Y^{3+}

B U^{3+}, V^{2+}, Y^{3+}

C Y^{3+}, U^{3+}, V^{2+}

D V^{2+}, Y^{3+}, U^{3+}

TABLE 3 Observations of metals in solutions of metallic ions

Trial number	Ion	Metal	Observation
1	U^{3+}	Y	Reaction
2	V^{2+}	U	Reaction
3	V^{2+}	Y	Reaction
4	Y^{3+}	V	No reaction

Short answer

6 The diagram in Figure 5 shows an electrochemical cell operating under standard conditions.

a **Construct** the equations occurring at the anode and cathode and the overall equation for the cell.

b **Identify** the oxidising agent.

c **Calculate** the standard reduction potential for Au. **Hint:** You should use the QCAA Chemistry formula and data book to answer this question.

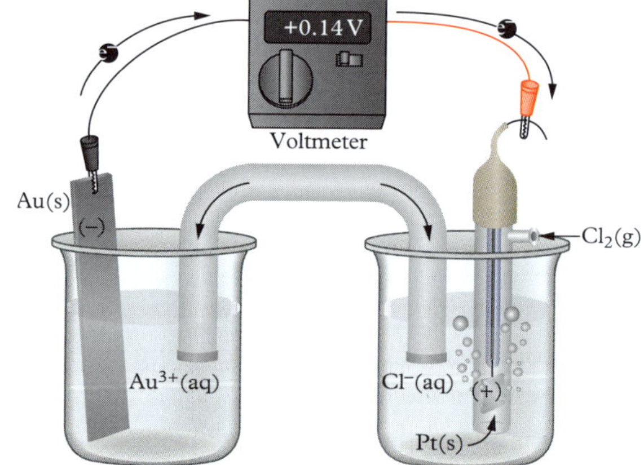

FIGURE 5 An electrochemical cell operating under standard conditions

7 **Use** the electrochemical series to **determine** if the following reactions occur spontaneously under standard conditions.

a $Ag^+(aq) + Fe^{2+}(aq) \rightarrow Ag(s) + Fe^{3+}(aq)$

b $Cu(s) + Pb^{2+}(aq) \rightarrow Cu^{2+}(aq) + Pb(s)$

8 **Use** the electrochemical series to **determine** if the following reactions occur spontaneously under standard conditions.

a $2Fe^{3+}(aq) + 2Br^-(aq) \rightarrow 2Fe^{2+}(aq) + Br_2(aq)$

b $2Cu^+(aq) \rightarrow Cu^{2+}(aq) + Cu(s)$

9 For the electrochemical cell in Figure 6:

a **Construct** the equations occurring at the anode and cathode and the overall equation for the cell in an acidic solution.

b **Calculate** the reading on the voltmeter of the cell (assuming standard conditions).

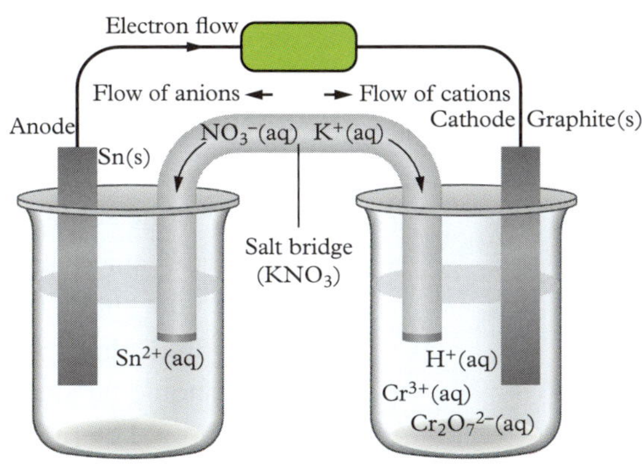

FIGURE 6 An electrochemical cell

10 A galvanic cell is formed by the combination of two half-cells: $X^{2+}(aq)/X(s)$ and $Ag^+(aq)/Ag(s)$, where X represents an unknown metal. When the cell is operating, the electron flow is as shown in Figure 7.

a **Deduce** in which half-cell the oxidation is occurring.

b **Construct** the equation for the oxidation half-cell, the equation for the reduction half-cell and the overall equation for the cell.

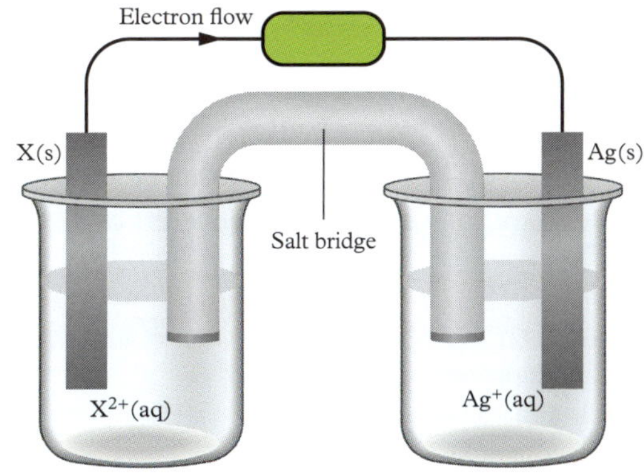

FIGURE 7 A galvanic cell

c **Identify** which electrode (X or Ag) is the anode.

d **Identify** which electrode (X or Ag) is the cathode.

e **Identify** which direction (towards X or towards Ag) the cations move through the salt bridge.

CHAPTER

Electrolytic cells

Electrolytic cells are the reverse of galvanic cells, where electrical energy is converted into chemical energy and it is a non-spontaneous reaction.

Electrolytic cells feature:

- An electrolyte solution that contains free moving ions. The ions donate or accept electrons, allowing them to 'flow' through the solution. An aqueous salt solution or a molten salt can be used.
- Two electrodes (the anode and cathode). Electrodes may be inert or metallic. The polarity of each electrode is dependent on whether they are attached to the positive or negative terminal of the power source.
- An external source of electrons (a battery or power source), which imposes the charge on an electrode in electrolysis.

During electrolysis, an external power source sends electrons to the cathode to cause reduction, so the cathode is now negative in polarity.

At the anode, an external power source removes the electrons to cause oxidation, so the anode is now positive.

The terms 'anion' and 'cation' are derived from electrolysis: anions (–) attracted to the anode (+), and cations (+) attracted to the cathode (–).

When predicting anode and cathode reactions, the species present at each electrode should be identified and then the strongest oxidant and strongest reductant would be predicted to react.

Applications of electrolysis include extraction and refinement of metals, chemical production, electroplating, water treatment, hair removal treatment and secondary cells (rechargeable batteries) for cars and mobile phones.

CHAPTER CHECKLIST

Read this checklist before you complete this chapter's activities, and then return to it to check your understanding before your assessments.

Once you have completed this chapter, you can use the 'I can …' statements to assess and rate your understanding of the topics covered by ticking the appropriate box in the 'rating column'.

I can …	Confidently	Partially	Not really
… understand electrolytic cells and construct redox half-equations for them.			
… explain how electrolytic cells are used in applications.			

DATA DRILL 8

Electrolysis experiments

A student used the following experimental set-up (Figure 1) to investigate the relationship between the current supplied by a power source and the time taken to deposit a specific amount of copper in an electrolysis experiment. The results are recorded in Table 1 below.

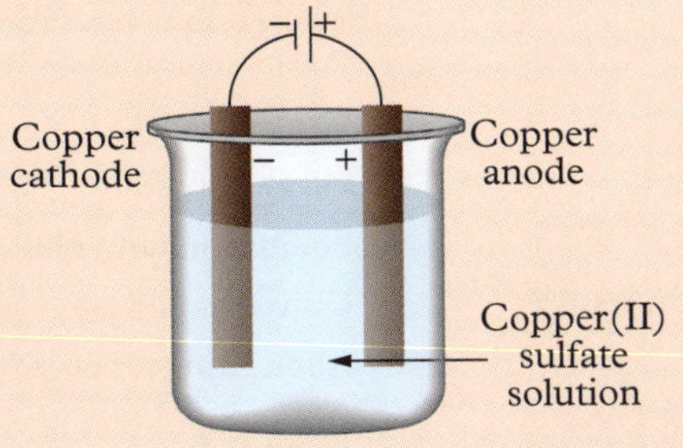

FIGURE 1 Standard set-up for an electrolysis experiment using copper

TABLE 1 Raw data collected from the electrolysis experiment

Experiment number	Average current (A)	Duration (min)
1	0.15	5
2	0.30	10
3	0.45	15
4	0.60	20
5	0.75	25
6	0.90	30

1 a **Construct** the redox equations occurring at the anode and the cathode for this experiment.

b **Create** a graph of the data in Table 1 to **identify** the relationship between average current and time.

EXPERIMENT EXPLORER 8

Constructing electrolytic cells

A class was divided into groups to construct an electrolytic cell using the materials in Table 2.

1 For the cell, **use** Figure 2 to **identify**:

- the anode and polarity (positive or negative)
- the cathode and polarity
- the movement of anions and cations
- the species present
- the oxidation and reduction equations
- the overall cell equation
- the theoretical minimum voltage required for a reaction using E° values from the electrochemical series.

TABLE 2 Materials used in the electrolytic cell

Electrolytic cell
Power source
Carbon electrodes
Glass U-tube
Sodium sulfate solution
Universal indicator
Connecting wires/clips

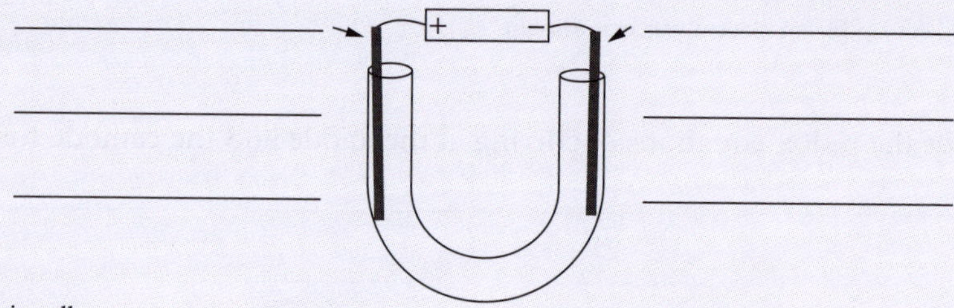

FIGURE 2 Electrolytic cell

RESEARCH REVIEW 8

Credible and non-credible resources

Electrolysis reactions are used in the extraction and refinement of metals, chemical production, electroplating, rust removal, water treatment, hair removal treatment and in rechargeable batteries for cars and mobile phones.

1 **Investigate** one of the applications mentioned above and **identify** one credible or non-credible resource on the use of electrolysis reactions. **Summarise** why it was or was not credible below.

Resource

Source:

Why was it credible or not?

EXAM EXCELLENCE 8

Multiple choice – circle the correct answer

1 A metal object is required to be silver-plated. Which one of the following statements best describes the electrolytic cell that could be used to produce an even plating of silver on the object?

A The object is connected to the negative terminal of an external power supply, a carbon rod is connected to the positive terminal, and both are placed in an aqueous solution of silver nitrate.

B The object is connected to the negative terminal of an external power supply, a silver rod is connected to the positive terminal, and both are placed in an aqueous solution of nitric acid.

C The object is connected to the positive terminal of an external power supply, a silver rod is connected to the negative terminal, and both are placed in an aqueous solution of silver nitrate.

D The object is connected to the negative terminal of an external power supply, a silver rod is connected to the positive terminal, and both are placed in an aqueous solution of silver nitrate.

2 The electrolytic cell in Figure 3 was constructed. The cathode reaction is:

A $2I^-(aq) \rightarrow I_2(g) + 2e^-$

B $Mg^{2+}(aq) + 2e^- \rightarrow Mg(s)$

C $2H_2O(l) \rightarrow 4H^+(aq) + O_2(g) + 4e^-$

D $2H_2O(l) + 2e^- \rightarrow H_2(g) + 2OH^-(aq)$

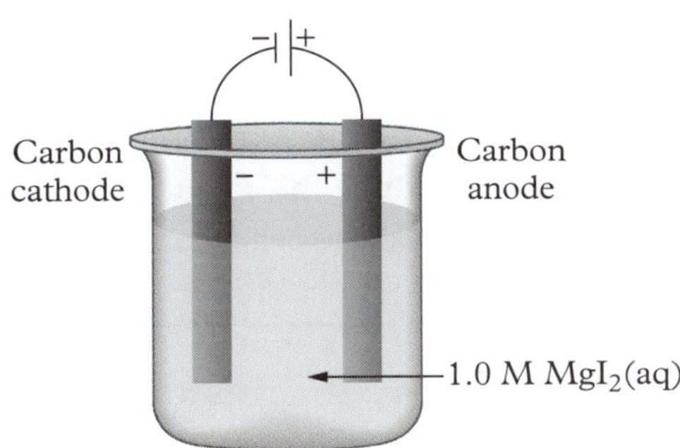

FIGURE 3 An electrolytic cell

3 What would be the product(s) produced at the cathode during the electrolysis of an aqueous solution of calcium nitrate using platinum electrodes?

A Calcium metal

B Hydrogen gas

C Hydrogen gas and hydroxide ions

D Oxygen gas and hydrogen ions

4 A molten binary salt, $ZnCl_2$, undergoes electrolysis. The half-reaction at the anode is:

A $Cl_2(g) + 2e^- \rightarrow 2Cl^-(aq)$

B $2Cl^-(aq) \rightarrow Cl_2(g) + 2e^-$

C $Zn^{2+}(aq) + 2e^- \rightarrow Zn(s)$

D $Ni(s) \rightarrow Ni^{2+}(aq) + 2e^-$

5 The industrial production of a sample of pure calcium would be best achieved by using:

A an electrolytic cell with molten calcium chloride as the electrolyte.

B an electrolytic cell with an aqueous solution of calcium chloride as the electrolyte.

C an electrolytic cell with a molten mixture of calcium chloride and sodium chloride as the electrolyte.

D an electrolytic cell with calcium oxide dissolved in molten cryolite as the electrolyte.

FIGURE 4 Pure calcium metal

Short answer

6 The following electrolytic cells in Figure 5 represent two different industrial applications.

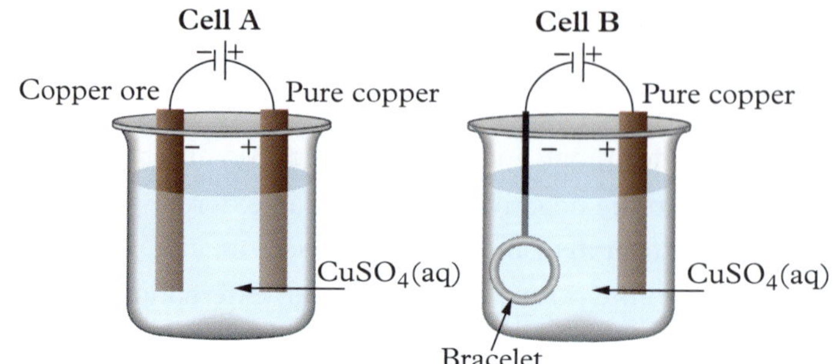

FIGURE 5 Electrolytic cells representing two industrial applications

a **Identify** the two industrial applications that these cells represent.

____

b **Consider** Cell B. At the initial stages of the reaction, the electrolyte $CuSO_4(aq)$ has a blue colour. **Deduce** the colour intensity of the electrolyte in Cell B (the same, increased or decreased) as the cell is functioning and **explain** your answer.

____

____

c **Consider** Cell A. **Infer** why the sludge formed at the bottom of Cell A is of economic importance.

____

____

7 Bromine can be prepared by the electrolysis of aqueous solutions of potassium bromide.

a **Determine** what materials would be used to construct the anode and cathode in an industrial-scale electrolytic cell to carry out this process.

____

b **Construct** the chemical half-equations for the reactions occurring at the anode and cathode during electrolysis. **Construct** the overall chemical equation for the electrolysis of an aqueous solution of potassium bromide.

____

____

____

8 A student set up the apparatus shown in Figure 6. The 9.0 V battery delivered a steady current of 2.0 A. Bubbles of gas were observed forming at both electrodes.

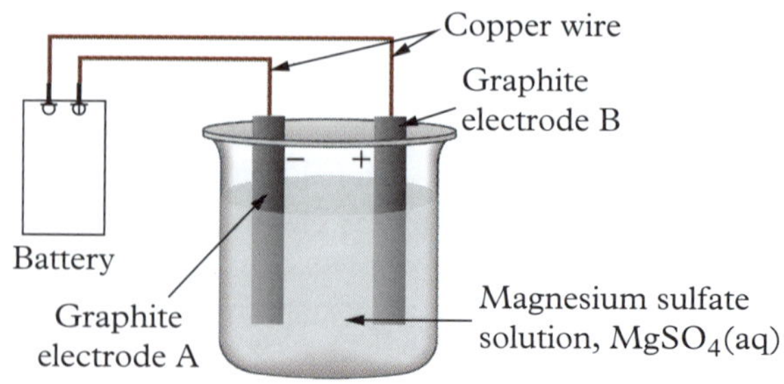

FIGURE 6 Experimental set-up of an electrolytic cell

a **Construct** a balanced half-equation for the reaction occurring at electrode A.

---

b **Deduce** the change expected (increased, decreased or unchanged) in the pH around electrode A after the cell had been operating. (**Hint: Consider** the change to H^+ ions.)

---

9 The following reaction takes place in a lead–acid storage battery:

$$2PbSO_4(s) + 2H_2O(l) \rightleftharpoons PbO_2(s) + Pb(s) + 2H_2SO_4(aq)$$

a **Construct** the balanced half-equations for the reactions at the anode and the cathode during the charging process.

---

b **Deduce** one advantage and one disadvantage of a lead–acid storage battery compared with a zinc–carbon battery.

---

10 A simplified diagram of a membrane cell used in the chlor-alkali industry is shown in Figure 7.

Gas A, Gas B and Compound C represent three products formed in this process. X and Y represent the cell electrodes.

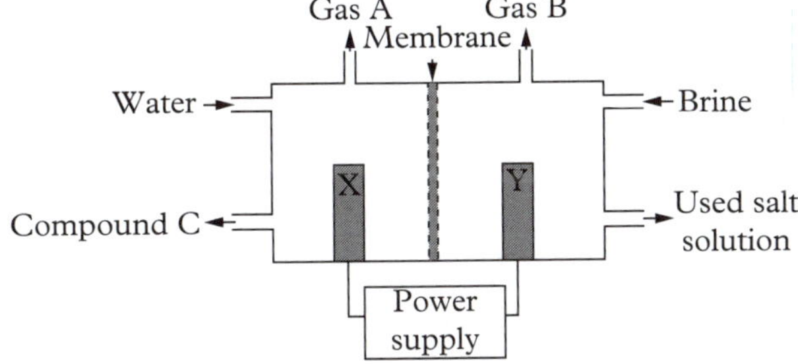

FIGURE 7 A simplified diagram of a membrane cell used in the chlor-alkali industry

a **Define** the function of the membrane in this cell.

---

b **Identify** the electrode that is connected to the positive terminal of the power supply and **explain** your response.

---

c **Identify** the names or formulas of Gas A, Gas B and Compound C in the above cell.

---

d **Construct** the balanced equations for the reactions occurring at the two electrodes and the net (or overall) reaction taking place in the cell.

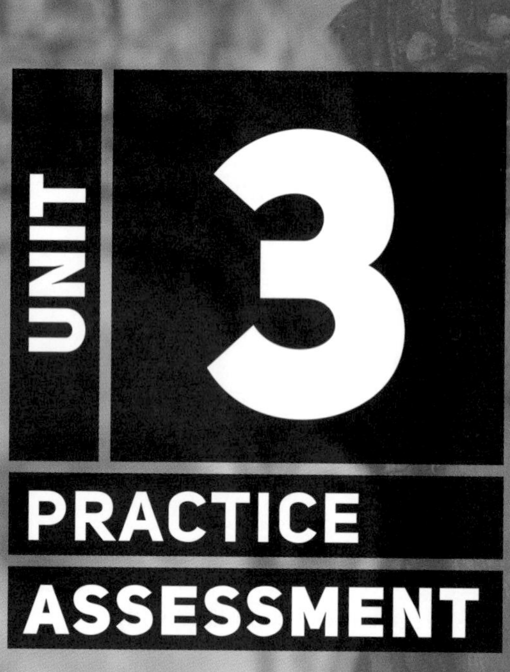

Equilibrium, acids and redox

Throughout the chapters in this unit you have practised analysing and recording data, conducting research and modifying experiments.

In this section, you will complete one of each of the following internal assessments:

- the Data test (10%)
- the Student experiment (20%)
- the Research investigation (20%).

Note: The assessments provided here are practice assessments. The final structure of each internal assessment will be set by the QCAA.

Unit 3 Data test

Dataset 1

The concentration of sodium hydroxide in waste water from an alumina refinery was to be determined by a student using volumetric analysis. Aliquots of 20.00 mL of the waste water were titrated against 0.150 M hydrochloric acid, using phenolphthalein as an indicator (Figure 1).

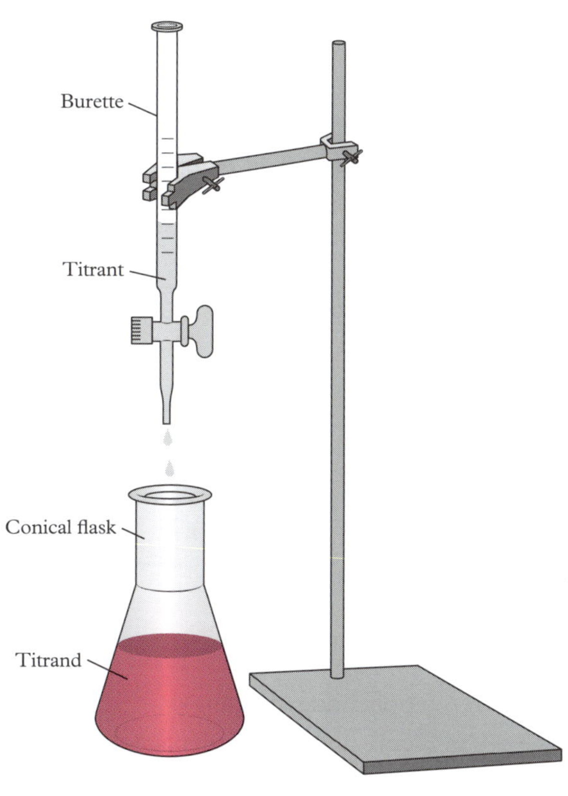

FIGURE 1 Experimental set-up for the titration

Results

The results of several titres are recorded in Table 1 below.

TABLE 1 Titres recorded for the above experiment

Titration number	1	2	3	4	5
Volume of titre (mL)	12.52	11.47	11.48	11.52	11.44

Item 1 (apply understanding)

- Determine the balanced chemical equation for the reaction, including the states.

2 marks

Item 2 (apply understanding)

- Calculate the average titre.

2 marks

Item 3 (analyse evidence)

- Identify a source of experimental error that is evident in the results of this experiment. Classify the source of error as random or systematic.

2 marks

Item 4 (apply understanding)

- Calculate the concentration of sodium hydroxide in the waste water.

2 marks

Item 5 (apply understanding)

- Calculate the mass of sodium hydroxide that would be present in 100 L of the waste water.

2 marks

Dataset 2

The line on the graph, in Figure 2 below, shows the concentrations at which butane and isobutane are at equilibrium at 25°C.

butane ⇌ isobutane

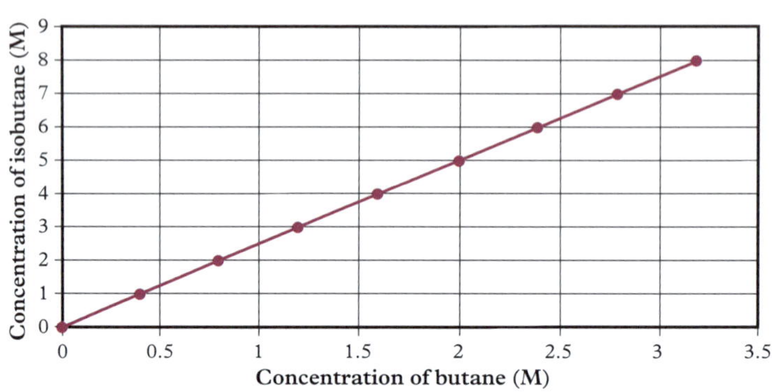

FIGURE 2 Relative concentrations of butane and isobutane at equilibrium (at 25°C)

Item 6 (apply understanding)

- Use Figure 2 above to calculate the equilibrium constant for the reaction at 25°C.

2 marks

Item 7 (apply understanding)

- If the equilibrium concentration of butane is 0.5 M:
  - **a** Sketch a point on the graph that represents the equilibrium at this concentration. Label this as point A.
  - **b** Sketch a point on the graph that indicates the relative concentrations of butane and isobutane at the time when 1.5 mol of butane is added. Label this as point B.

2 marks

Item 8 (analyse data)

- Consider the reaction quotient (Q) at the time when the butane was added. Deduce whether the value of the equilibrium constant (K) would be greater than or less than Q and justify your answer.

3 marks

Item 9 (analyse data)

- Consider the system at point B. Equilibrium is restored at point C when [butane] = 0.93 M and [isobutane] = 2.32 M.

  Identify this point on your graph and label it as point C. If points C and B were connected, the line would have a gradient of –1. Identify a reason for this observation.

3 marks

Unit 3 Student experiment

Your task is to modify the following experiment. Please note that you must conduct a risk assessment before conducting this experiment. See page 60. This is a requirement of the Student experiment.

3.7 Measuring pH

Aim

To identify the pH level of different substances by using pH indicators, pH test papers and a pH meter.

Materials

- pH indicators (e.g. methyl orange, methyl red etc.)
- Universal indicator
- Litmus paper (blue or red)
- pH meter
- Vinegar
- Milk
- Lemon juice
- Bleach
- Lemonade
- Shampoo
- Deionised water
- Beakers

Method

1 Pour each liquid into a separate beaker.
2 Measure the pH of each liquid with all of the available pH indicators.
3 Record your observations and measurements in Table 2 below.

Results

Table 1 shows some example results for the experiment.

TABLE 1 pH measurements of different substances

Substance	Observations and pH measurements				
	Methyl red	Litmus paper (blue)	Litmus paper (red)	Universal indicator	pH meter
Vinegar	Red	Red	Red	Pink	2.8
Milk	Yellow	Blue	Blue	Green	6.5
Lemon juice	Red	Red	Red	Pink	2.4
Bleach	Yellow	Blue	Blue	Violet or indigo	12.0
Lemonade	Red	Red	Red	Pink	3.2
Shampoo	Red	Red	Red	Pink	5.7
Deionised water	Yellow	Blue	Red	Green	7.0

Modification of the original experiment

Note: This section provides prompts for your modification. You may require extra space to write your full practice assessment.

Aim

Research question

Background research

Methodology

Results

Discussion (rationale)

Risk assessment

Name: ______________________________

Experiment title: ____

Note: Risks should be managed by the use of personal protective equipment and/or specified control measures. Always consult your teacher before conducting an experiment.

Equipment required

____

____

____

____

____

____

Hazardous chemicals required and produced

Reactant or product name and concentration	GHS classification	GHS hazard statement	Control measures

Non-hazardous substances

Reactant or product name and concentration	GHS classification	GHS hazard statement	Control measures

Other hazards and possible risks

Protective measures

Lab coat	Safety glasses	Gloves	Fume cupboard	Other

Clean up and disposal of wastes

Teacher's signature: ______________________

Student's signature: ______________________

Date: ______________________

Note: This assessment is not valid until it has been completed and signed by your teacher.

Unit 3 Research investigation

Note: The Research investigation (IA3) is completed in Unit 4 and covers content from Unit 4. There is no assessable Research investigation during Unit 3. This Research investigation has been included for you to practise the skills required for the Unit 4 assessment.

CASE STUDY

Ocean acidification: what are the impacts?

Carbon dioxide makes up 0.035% of our atmosphere, which directly or indirectly provides food for all living species through the process of photosynthesis. Carbon dioxide is consumed through photosynthesis and then re-released to the atmosphere through respiration in plants and animals. However, other ways that carbon dioxide can return to the atmosphere include waste or dead animal decomposition, volcanic activity and combustion of fossil fuels. Currently the atmospheric levels of carbon dioxide are increasing due to burning fossil fuels.

Because carbon dioxide is soluble in water, it is rapidly dissolved by the oceans, generating carbonic acid. As the amount of carbon dioxide in the atmosphere increases, more dissolves into the ocean, increasing the ocean's acidity. This increasing acidity is gradually affecting the marine environment and species that inhabit the oceans (Figure 1) and may eventually lead to further social and economic impacts on coastal communities.

FIGURE 1 An example of the before- (left) and after-effects (right) of ocean acidification on the Great Barrier Reef in the form of coral bleaching.

Your task is to conduct a Research investigation about the following claim, which is related to the case study above:

Oceans acting as a carbon dioxide sink are increasing in acidification, which can impact the environment, marine species and coastal society.

Research question

Research

Note: This section provides space for you to investigate two sources; you will need to research further to complete the assessment.

Resource 1

- Title:
- Author(s):
- Source and credibility:
- Publication date:
- Aim:
- Resource's research question:
- Methodology
  - What data was collected?
  - How was the data collected?
- Results
  - Did the resource support your research question?
  - Why does/doesn't it support the provided claim?

Resource 2

- Title:
- Author(s):
- Source and credibility:
- Publication date:
- Aim:
- Resource's research question:
- Methodology
  - What data was collected?
  - How was the data collected?
- Results
  - Did the resource support your research question?
  - Why does/doesn't it support the provided claim?

Planning your internal assessment

Structure, synthesis and design

PRACTICALS IN THIS UNIT

	SUGGESTED PRACTICAL	**9.3** Interpreting 2D and 3D functional groups
	MANDATORY PRACTICAL	**9.4** Modelling isomers of organic molecules
	SUGGESTED PRACTICAL	**10.1** Bromination of unsaturated hydrocarbons (TEACHER-ONLY DEMONSTRATION)
	SUGGESTED PRACTICAL	**10.2** Oxidation of alcohols (TEACHER-ONLY DEMONSTRATION)
	SUGGESTED PRACTICAL	**11.3** Catalysing decomposition reactions
	SUGGESTED PRACTICAL	**12.1** Identifying amino acids by paper chromatography
	SUGGESTED PRACTICAL	**12.2** Using mass spectrometry and infrared spectroscopy to identify organic compounds
	SUGGESTED PRACTICAL	**13.1A** Haber process simulation using Wolfram
	SUGGESTED PRACTICAL	**13.1B** Video simulation of the contact process

WORD WIZARD

Draw a line to match each term with the correct definition.

HALOALKANE	a class of organic compound that has a carbonyl group on a carbon within the main chain
HYDROCARBON	a complex sugar consisting of multiple sugar monomers bonded together
CATALYST	a class of organic compound that contains a halogen substituent
BIODEGRADATION	replaceable at a rate equal to or greater than the rate of use, over an indefinite period
RENEWABLE	a substance at a temperature and pressure beyond its critical point, where the substance has properties of both a gas and liquid
MASS SPECTROMETRY	the production of very concentrated sulfuric acid
KETONE	a technique used to determine the molecular weight of a compound
AMIDE	a single unit within a polymer
ESTERIFICATION	the bond joining amino acid monomers together, between the carboxyl and amine groups of adjacent amino acids
MOLECULAR MANUFACTURING	the atomically precise placement of atoms or molecules in order to build larger molecular assemblies or molecular-based machines
SUPERCRITICAL FLUID	an organic compound consisting of only carbon and hydrogen atoms
HABER PROCESS	a substance that increases the rate of a reaction without itself being consumed in the reaction
MONOMER	electromagnetic radiation in the region between visible light and microwave radiation
POLYSACCHARIDE	a class of organic compound that contains amine and carbonyl functional groups adjacent to each other
CONTACT PROCESS	a nitrogen fixation process to produce ammonia
INFRARED RADIATION	the breakdown of a substance, such as plastic, by microorganisms
PEPTIDE BOND	a condensation reaction between a carboxylic acid and alcohol that generates an ester

CHAPTER 9

Structure of organic compounds

Organic chemistry is the chemistry of carbon compounds, many of which form a homologous series or compounds of the same type. Carbon forms strong, stable covalent bonds with itself and other elements (such as H, O, N, Cl, F, I, Br and S). There are clear naming rules set by the International Union of Pure and Applied Chemistry (IUPAC). Organic compounds form isomers, which have the same molecular formula but different structural arrangements, giving different physical and chemical properties to each compound in a homologous series.

Stereoisomers have the same molecular and structural formula but different spatial arrangements. Geometric isomers are defined by the substituent group arrangement around a rigid C=C bond: *cis* isomers have similar substituent groups on the same side or plane, above or below; *trans* isomers have similar substituent groups on the opposite side, above and below. Enantiomers are isomers defined by the four substituent arrangements (tetrahedral) around a chiral carbon atom with non-superimposable mirror images.

Physical and chemical properties of organic compounds with functional groups in any homologous series are influenced by the size of the substituent group (R) attached. Larger substituent groups have increased intermolecular attractions, melting points, boiling points and viscosity of compounds. Amino acids, comprised of amine ($-NH_2$) and carboxyl ($-COOH$) functional groups, are the main components of proteins, genes and DNA.

CHAPTER CHECKLIST

Read this checklist before you complete this chapter's activities, then return to it to check your understanding before your assessments.

Once you have completed this chapter, you can use the 'I can …' statements to assess and rate your understanding of the topics covered by ticking the appropriate box in the 'rating column'.

I can …	Confidently	Partially	Not really
… understand the different bonding in hydrocarbons.			
… identify the different organic compounds containing oxygen or nitrogen.			
… explain the difference between extended, condensed and line structural formulas.			
… explain what stereoisomers are.			
… describe the physical properties of organic compounds.			

RESEARCH REVIEW 9

Oral presentations

Biotechnology applications are used for disease detection, development of new and personalised pharmaceutical treatments, biofuels, textiles, genetically modified and sustainable food crops, bioremediation or environmental applications, forensic investigation, and also in paper, plastic, personal care and detergent manufacturing.

1 **Select** one of the applications mentioned above and **create** a three-minute speech to present to the class (Figure 1). This can be done as a group. **Use** the space below to **summarise** your research and brainstorm ideas.

FIGURE 1 Oral presentations are an optional method for presenting both the Student experiment and Research investigation.

Study tip

When naming organic compounds according to the IUPAC rules, avoid common errors including not identifying the longest carbon chain, not listing the side branches in alphabetical order or not including the multipliers 'di', 'tri' and 'tetra'.

EXAM EXCELLENCE 9

Multiple choice – circle the correct answer

1 Which one of the following groups of compounds is a homologous series?

A CH_3-OH $\quad CH_3-C(=O)-OH$ $\quad CH_3CH_2-C(=O)-OH$

B $CH_3-C(CH_3)_2-Cl$ $\quad CH_3-C(CH_3)_2-Br$ $\quad CH_3-C(CH_3)_2-I$

C $CH_3-CH(CH_3)-OH$ $\quad CH_3-C(CH_3)(CH_3)-OH$ $\quad CH_3-C(CH_3)(CH_2CH_3)-OH$

D CH_3CH_2Cl $\quad CH_3CHCl_2$ $\quad CH_3CCl_3$

2 What is the name of the compound with the following structural formula?

A Acetamide

B Formyl acetamide

C Dimethyl acetate

D *N*,*N*-Dimethylformamide

$(CH_3)_2NCH(=O)$

FIGURE 2 Structural formula of an unknown compound

3 Which of the following substances is the least soluble in water?

A $H-CH_2-O-H$ (H–C(H)(H)–O–H)

B $H-CH_2-CH_2-O-H$ (H–C(H)(H)–C(H)(H)–O–H)

C $CH_3CH_2C(=O)OH$

D $CH_3C(=O)OCH_3$

4 Which of the molecules shown below is a structural isomer of pentene?

A $CH_3-CH_2-CH_2-CH_2-CH_3$

B $CH_3-CH_2-CH(OH)-CH_2-CH_3$

C $CH_3-CH=CH-CH_3$

D $CH_3-C(CH_3)=CH-CH_3$

5 The IUPAC name for the following compound is:

A 4-ethyl-*cis*-3-octene

B 4-ethyl-*trans*-3-octene

C 4-butyl-*cis*-3-hexene

D 5-ethyl-*trans*-5-octene

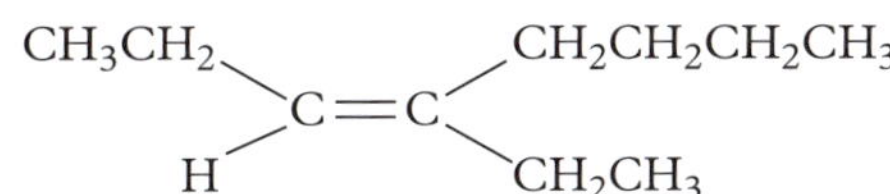

FIGURE 3 Structural formula of an unknown compound

Short answer

6 The graph in Figure 4 below shows the boiling points of alkanes, alcohols and carboxylic acids with one to four carbon atoms.

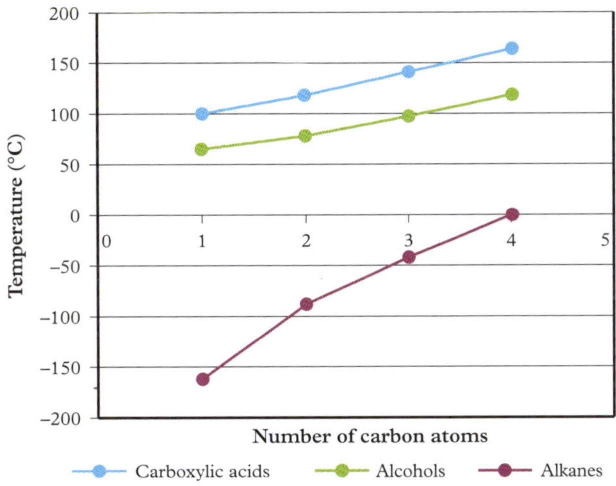

FIGURE 4 The boiling points of alkanes, alcohols and carboxylic acids with one to four carbon atoms

a **Explain** why the boiling points of the alkanes are much lower than the boiling points of the alcohols and the carboxylic acids.

______

______

______

______

______

b **Explain** why the boiling points of all three series of compounds increase with increasing numbers of carbon atoms.

______

______

______

______

______

7 **Identify** the missing information in Table 1 below.

TABLE 1 Names and formulas of some organic compounds

Name	Extended structural formula
Propan-2-ol	
Hexanoic acid	
Hept-3-yne	
1,1,1-Trifluoroethane	
	H–C(H)(H)–C(H)(H)–C(OH)(H)–C(H)(H)–C(H)(H)–C(H)(H)–C(H)(H)–H
2-Chloro-2,5-dibromo-3-methyl-hept-3-ene	

8 The experimental results of the miscibility with water for some substances are shown in Table 2. **Explain** these observations.

TABLE 2 Observations of the miscibility with water for some substances

Substance	Observations
Hexane (C_6H_{14})	Did not dissolve
Hexene (C_6H_{12})	Did not dissolve
Ethanol (CH_3CH_2OH)	Did dissolve
Propanoic acid (CH_3CH_2COOH)	Did dissolve

9 a **Deduce** the number of chiral carbon atoms in the following molecules.

i CH_3 / H_3C / H / CH_3

ii CO_2H / H—OH / H—OH / CO_2H

iii OH / CH_3

b **Deduce** whether the following pairs of compounds are geometric isomers, enantiomers or the same compound.

i

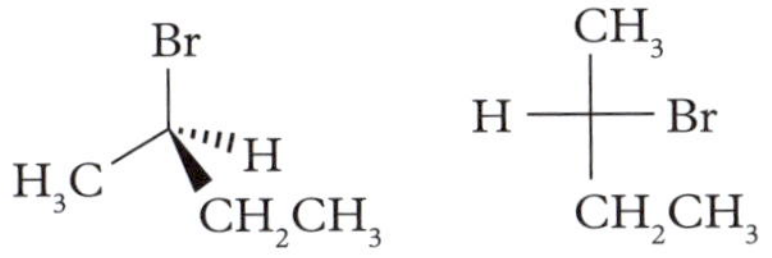

ii

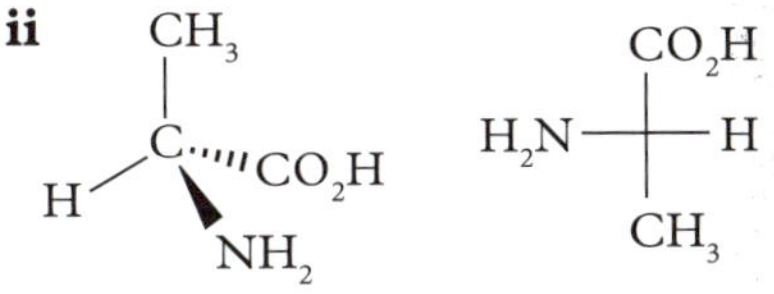

iii

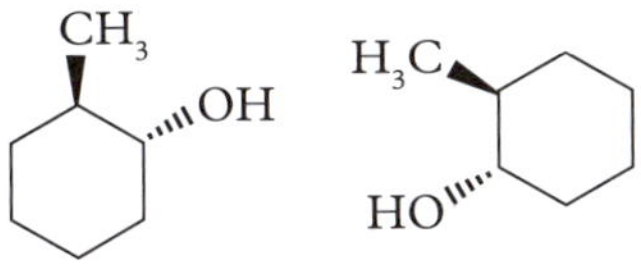

10 **Construct** the possible isomers for C_7H_{17} and **use** IUPAC rules to name them.

Organic reactions and reaction pathways

Different types of organic compounds can be formed from simple unsaturated hydrocarbons by different reactions. There are different types of addition reactions, including hydrogenation, halogenation, hydrohalogenation, hydration and polymerisation.

Oxidation reactions occur in primary and secondary alcohols, and colour-changing reagents can be used to determine whether the alcohol undergoing oxidation is a primary, secondary or tertiary alcohol. Reduction reactions occur in conjunction with oxidation reactions.

There are two types of condensation reactions that are particularly important: carboxylic acids that react with alcohols to form esters (esterification) using sulfuric acid as a catalyst, and carboxylic acids that react with amines to form amides, in the presence of heat.

There are different types of substitution reactions. These include alkanes being substituted with halogens in the presence of sunlight or UV light to form haloalkanes. Haloalkanes can also be substituted by using heat and a solution of potassium cyanide and ethanol to form nitriles; by using heat, sodium hydroxide and an ethanol/water solvent mixture to form alcohols; by using sodium iodide (for example) and ethanol (or an organic solvent) to form haloalkanes; or by using heat and a concentrated ammonia/ethanol solution to form amines.

CHAPTER CHECKLIST

Read this checklist before you complete this chapter's activities, then return to it to check your understanding before your assessments.

Once you have completed this chapter, you can use the 'I can …' statements to assess and rate your understanding of the topics covered by ticking the appropriate box in the 'rating column'.

I can …	Confidently	Partially	Not really
… identify the different addition and elimination reactions.			
… identify the different oxidation and reduction reactions.			
… identify esterification and amide synthesis reactions.			
… identify the substitution of alkanes and haloalkanes.			

RESEARCH REVIEW 10

Writing a research question

The following claim was suggested about green polymers (Figure 1):

Green polymers are produced from renewable resources and have a smaller ecological footprint than that of other synthetic polymers.

1 **Identify** the key terms in the claim.

2 **Define** the key terms.

3 **Create** two research questions for this claim.

FIGURE 1 Recycled plastic forms these green granules.

EXAM EXCELLENCE 10

Multiple choice – circle the correct answer

1 A polymer, used to stitch wounds, is made from a condensation polymerisation reaction between lactic acid (HOCH)(CH_3)COOH, and glycolic acid. The formula of glycolic acid is:

A $HOCH_2COOH$

B $HOCH_2CH_2OH$

C $HOOCCH_2COOH$

D $HOOCCH_2CH_2OH$

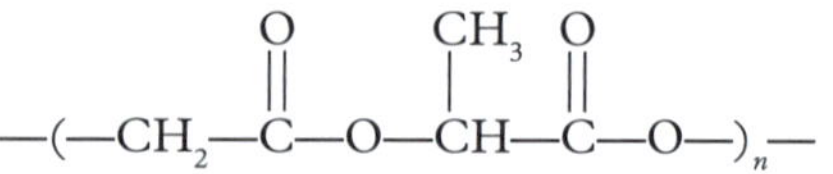

FIGURE 2 A biodegradable polymer

2 Liquid bromine Br_2 dissolves in unsaturated hydrocarbons and reacts immediately. Which statement below best describes this process?

A Bromine is polar and reacts by adding bromine atoms across the double bond.

B Bromine is polar and reacts by substituting hydrogen atoms with bromine atoms.

C Bromine is non-polar and reacts by substituting hydrogen atoms with bromine atoms.

D Bromine is non-polar and reacts by adding bromine atoms across the double bond.

Questions 3 and 4 relate to the following three reactions:

Reaction 1: $X + KOH(aq) \rightarrow CH_3CH_2OH(l) + KCl(aq)$

Reaction 2: $CH_3CH_2OH(l) \xrightarrow{Y} CH_3COOH(l)$

Reaction 3: $CH_3COOH(l) + CH_3OH(l) \rightarrow Z + H_2O(l)$

3 Which of the following shows the formulas of species X, Y and Z?

	Species X	Species Y	Species Z
A	CH_3CH_2Cl	H_2O/H^+	CH_3COCH_3
B	CH_3CH_2Cl	$K_2Cr_2O_7/H^+$	CH_3COOCH_3
C	CH_2ClCH_2Cl	H_2O/H^+	CH_3COOCH_3
D	CH_2ClCH_2Cl	$K_2Cr_2O_7/H^+$	CH_3COCH_3

4 Which of the following correctly identifies each reaction type?

	Reaction 1	Reaction 2	Reaction 3
A	Substitution	Oxidation	Condensation
B	Addition	Oxidation	Reduction
C	Substitution	Elimination	Reduction
D	Addition	Elimination	Condensation

5 In the following chemical reactions, predict which one would form more than two products:

A The condensation of methanol and ethanoic acid

B The acid-catalysed hydration of but-2-ene

C The chlorination of ethane in the presence of sunlight

D The catalysed addition of hydrogen bromide to ethene.

Short answer

6 **a** **Construct** the chemical equation for the substitution reaction between $CH_3CHClCH_3$ and NH_3.

____

b **Apply** the IUPAC rules to name the molecule formed.

____

7 **Identify** and complete the missing information in the following flow chart in Figure 3.

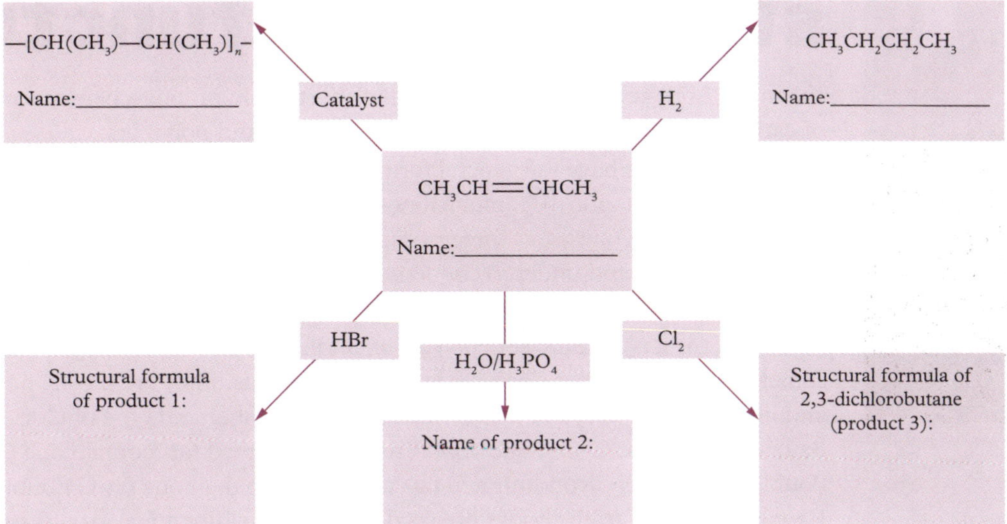

FIGURE 3 A flow chart showing different reactions

8 Two reactions of an alkene B are shown below in Figure 4.

$$\underset{\mathbf{A}}{C_4H_{10}} \xleftarrow[\text{Ni}]{H_2} \underset{\mathbf{B}}{CH_3(H)C{=}C(H)CH_3} \longrightarrow \underset{\mathbf{C}}{C_4H_9Br}$$

FIGURE 4 Two reactions of an alkene B

a **Construct** a chemical equation for the complete combustion of A.

____

b **Construct** a chemical equation for the conversion of B to C.

____

9 The polymer TEFLON®™ is made by the polymerisation of the monomer shown in Figure 5.

a **Apply** the IUPAC rules to name this monomer and the polymer that it forms.

____

b **Identify** the type of polymerisation occurring.

____

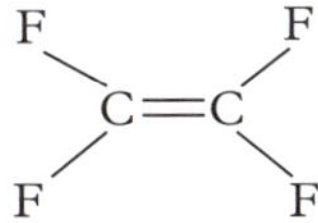

FIGURE 5 Monomer used to form the polymer TEFLON®™

10 From the starting reagents of ethene ($CH_2{=}CH_2$) and propane ($CH_3CH_2CH_3$), **construct** a reaction pathway diagram to form the product ethyl propanoate ($CH_3CH_2COOCH_2CH_3$).

CHAPTER 11

Organic materials: structure and function

Examples of organic materials include the short-chain or long-chain macromolecules of carbohydrates, lipids, fats, triglycerides, proteins and polymers.

Carbohydrates have the general formula $C_n(H_2O)_n$ and a molecular mass range between 100 and 10^6 amu. Monosaccharides (or sugars) have a general formula of $C_6H_{12}O_6$, exist as three isomers (a straight chain or α-ring or β-ring) in water, taste sweet and undergo condensation reactions to form disaccharides and polysaccharides.

Lipids (or fats) mainly contain carbon and hydrogen, some oxygen and may sometimes contain other elements in smaller amounts. They are mostly non-polar and insoluble in water, and are identified by the number and type of C–C bonds. Saturated fats have C-C single bonds, monounsaturated fats contain one C=C double bond, and polyunsaturated fats contain more than one C=C double bond. Base hydrolysis of triglycerides breaks down the ester functional groups to form glycerol and fatty acid salts (soap).

Proteins contain monomers called amino acids. They have the amino group, the carboxyl group and an R group all on the same carbon atom. They exist in different forms, but in neutral pH they form zwitterions. Protein primary structures involve the sequence or order of amino acids joined through condensation reactions to form peptide bonds; secondary structures involve twisting of amino acid chains to form 3D shapes (α-helixes or β-sheets) held together by hydrogen bonds between the –NH and C=O groups; and tertiary structures are the overall three-dimensional shape of a protein.

Polymers are most often made from fossil fuel derivatives, such as alkene compounds containing the C=C bond by addition or condensation polymerisation. Scientists are now working on the manufacture of biodegradable or more environmentally sustainable polymers sourced from natural or renewable resources.

CHAPTER CHECKLIST

Read this checklist before you complete this chapter's activities, then return to it to check your understanding before your assessments.

Once you have completed this chapter, you can use the 'I can …' statements to assess and rate your understanding of the topics covered by ticking the appropriate box in the 'rating column'.

I can …	Confidently	Partially	Not really
… define different carbohydrates.			
… define different lipids.			
… define different proteins.			
… describe how synthetic polymers are formed.			

RESEARCH REVIEW 11

Selecting a strong research question

Organic-based compounds (such as organochlorines, organophosphates, nicotine, carbamates, arsenates and cyanides) have been used as insecticides and pesticides for many decades (Figure 1). Some have structures that target enzymes or proteins in neurotransmitters of insects to disrupt or accelerate their metabolic functions.

FIGURE 1 Insecticides being sprayed on vegetables

1 Two research questions have been formulated below. **Determine** which question is stronger and why.

Question 1: 'Are organic-based compounds good insecticides and pesticides?'

Question 2: 'What organic components of nicotine are effective as an insecticide?'

2 **Use** the space below to **construct** a research plan for the stronger question. Include all the steps required to prepare you for a Research investigation.

EXAM EXCELLENCE 11

Multiple choice – circle the correct answer

1 Cellulose is an example of a:

A Monosaccharide

B Disaccharide

C Polysaccharide

D Alcohol.

2 Saponification:

A involves boiling triglycerides with excess aqueus sodium hydroxide, to break three ester linkages.

B involves the breakdown of organic material through microorganisms.

C involves the reaction between water and an organic compound in the presence of a catalyst.

D involves the addition of hydrogen across a multiple bond.

3 The functional group that forms when glycerol reacts with a fatty acid can be represented by which of the following diagram?

A
:O:
||
—C—Ö—

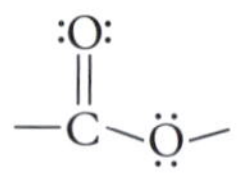

B
—C—Ö—C—

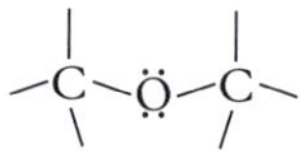

C
:O:
||
—C—N̈—
|
H

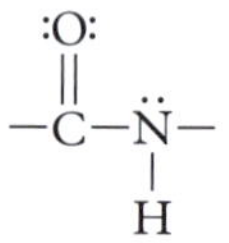

D
—C—Ö—Ö—C—

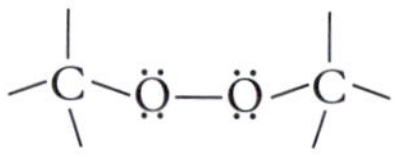

4 In response to a pain stimulus, the brain produces small polypeptide molecules called enkephalins. These molecules block the transmission of pain through the central nervous system.
The amino acid sequence in one such compound, methionine enkephalin, is:

Tyr – Gly – Gly – Phe – Met

The number of amine, carboxylic acid and amide (peptide) functional groups in this polypeptide is:

	$-NH_2$	–COOH	–CONH
A	0	0	5
B	1	1	4
C	1	1	5
D	0	2	4

5 Stearic acid ($C_{17}H_{35}COOH$) is a fatty acid derived from animal fats, whereas linoleic acid ($C_{17}H_{31}COOH$) is a fatty acid derived from vegetable oil. The melting point of stearic acid is predicted to be higher than linoleic acid because:

A the hydrogen bonds between molecules of stearic acid are stronger as a consequence of the greater number of hydrogen atoms present.

B stearic acid has a saturated hydrocarbon chain, compared with linoleic acid that has an unsaturated hydrocarbon chain.

C the greater number of hydrogen atoms increases the relative molecular mass and hence significantly increases the dispersion forces between the molecules.

D the strength of the C–C bonds in linoleic acid are less than those in stearic acid.

Short answer

6 **Construct** the general structure of an amino acid in the zwitterion form, clearly showing all bonds and ionic charges.

7 **Identify** the purpose that enzymes serve in chemical reactions. **Contrast** the key difference in the way enzymes operate with that of inorganic catalysts (such as Ni).

8 **Describe** the primary and secondary structures of proteins.

9 **Identify** the class of carbohydrates that includes maltose, sucrose and lactose.

10 Fats and oils in foods are made up of complex mixtures of saturated and unsaturated fatty acids. An example is a vegetable oil, which is shown in Figure 2.

A student in Brisbane wanted to make their own handmade soap from this vegetable oil.

Construct the equation for the base hydrolysis of this vegetable oil to form a soap and **identify** the type of reaction.

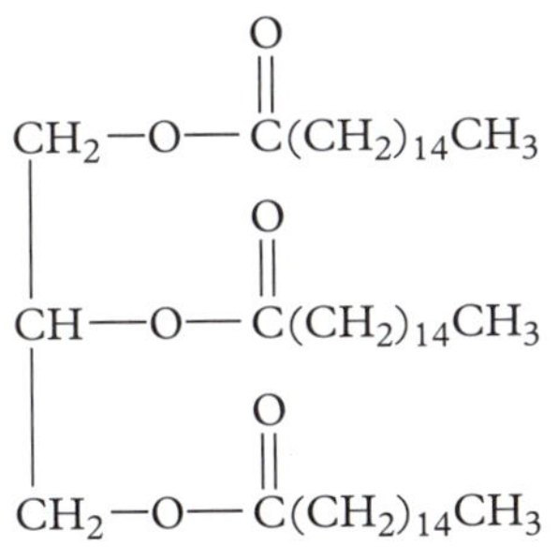

$CH_2-O-C(=O)(CH_2)_{14}CH_3$

$CH-O-C(=O)(CH_2)_{14}CH_3$

$CH_2-O-C(=O)(CH_2)_{14}CH_3$

FIGURE 2 Structure of a vegetable oil

CHAPTER 12

Analytical techniques

Proteins are separated according to their size, charge and binding strength to other molecules. Two specific protein separation techniques are size exclusion chromatography and electrophoresis. Size exclusion chromatography separates different-sized proteins in gel volume fractions through a column.

Electrophoresis or PAGE (polyacrylamide gel electrophoresis) separates proteins through a gel in an applied electric field by opposite charges being attracted to electrodes.

Mass spectrometry uses ionisation and high-energy electron bombardment to create positive ions of gaseous samples, with variable mass to charge (m/z) ratios, which are deflected by a magnetic field onto a detector to produce a mass spectrum. The 'rule of 13' and base value from the m/z ratio of the molecular ion formed can determine its molecular formula.

Infrared spectroscopy measures the absorbance of infrared radiation of specific chemical bonds in a sample that correspond to the same frequency as their natural bending and stretching vibration(s). The frequency of the vibrations, measured in wavenumbers (cm^{-1}), depends on the masses of the atoms involved and their bond lengths.

X-ray crystallography measures the amount of scattering of x-ray radiation after bombardment of a crystal or solid sample, which is proportional to the number of electrons present.

CHAPTER CHECKLIST

Read this checklist before you complete this chapter's activities, then return to it to check your understanding before your assessments.

Once you have completed this chapter, you can use the 'I can …' statements to assess and rate your understanding of the topics covered by ticking the appropriate box in the 'rating column'.

I can …	Confidently	Partially	Not really
… describe how size exclusion chromatography and electrophoresis separate proteins.			
… explain how mass spectrometry works.			
… explain how infrared spectroscopy works.			
… explain how x-ray crystallography works.			

RESEARCH REVIEW 12

Credible and non-credible resources

The analytical techniques summarised in this chapter can be used in many industries, including:

- forensic analysis
- manufacturing of polymers (for measuring the degree of polymerisation)
- food industry, pesticide testing and allergen testing (for quality control)
- space industry (for tracking hydrocarbons in the universe, Figure 1)
- geology industry (for detecting oil deposits and other minerals in rocks).

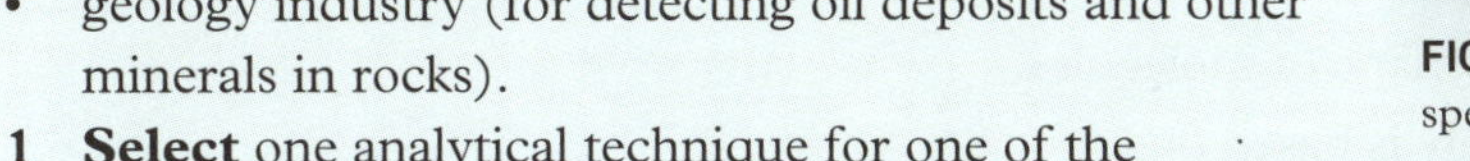

FIGURE 1 The space industry uses mass spectrometry to track hydrocarbons in space.

1 **Select** one analytical technique for one of the industries mentioned above and **identify** one credible resource and one non-credible resource on the use of the analytical technique. **Summarise** why they were or were not credible below.

Resource 1

Source:

Why was it credible or not?

Resource 2

Source:

Why was it credible or not?

EXAM EXCELLENCE 12

Multiple choice – circle the correct answer

1 In size exclusion chromatography:

A the largest molecule is eluted first.
B the smallest molecule is eluted first.
C the highest charged molecule is eluted first.
D size is excluded from the separation of the proteins.

2 In electrophoresis, the speed of migration of proteins in an electric field depends on:

A the magnitude (size) of charge and mass of molecules.
B the magnitude of charge and shape of molecules.
C the shape and size of molecules.
D the magnitude of charge, size and shape of molecules.

3 The technique of infrared spectroscopy is based on:

A the nuclei of different atoms being affected by the nuclei of adjoining atoms.
B the bonds between different atoms in molecules absorbing different wavelengths of energy.
C the bonds between different atoms in a molecule emitting different wavelengths of light when excited.
D the bonds between different hydrogen atoms in a molecule absorbing different wavelengths of light.

4 The diagram in Figure 2 represents the mass spectrum of a pure sample.

Deduce which one of the following pure samples is most likely to produce this spectrum.

A Ethanol
B Propan-1-ol
C Butan-1-ol
D Pentan-1-ol

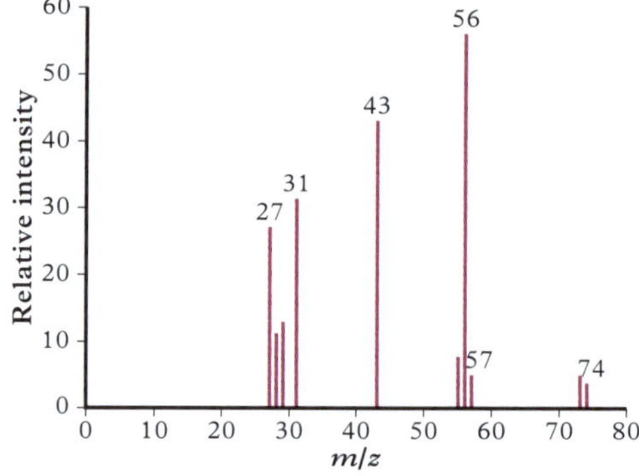

FIGURE 2 Mass spectrum of a pure sample

5 What is the role of sodium dodecyl sulfate (SDS) in SDS PAGE?

A Protein denaturing and to convey a net negative charge
B To convey an overall negative charge to the protein
C To give equal mass to all proteins
D Protein unfolding and to convey a net positive charge

Short answer

6 Interpolate the data in the size exclusion chromatography calibration curve in Figure 3 to **determine** the estimated molecular weight of an unknown protein with a retention volume of 3.2 mL.

____

____

____

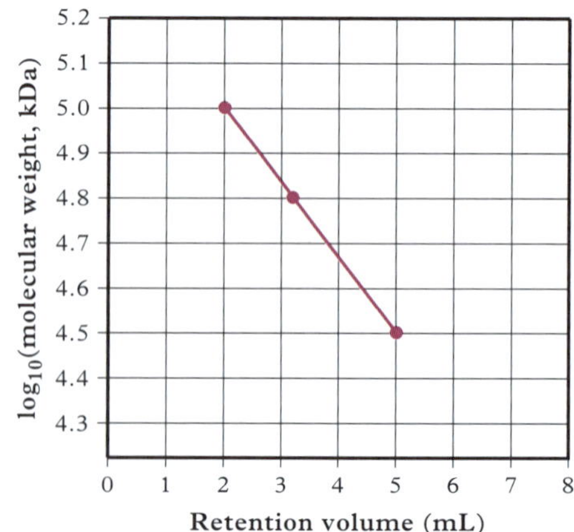

FIGURE 3 Size exclusion chromatography calibration curve of an unknown protein

7 An organic compound was analysed and found to contain 48.6% carbon, 8.2% hydrogen and 43.2% oxygen. **Deduce** the empirical formula of this compound.

____

____

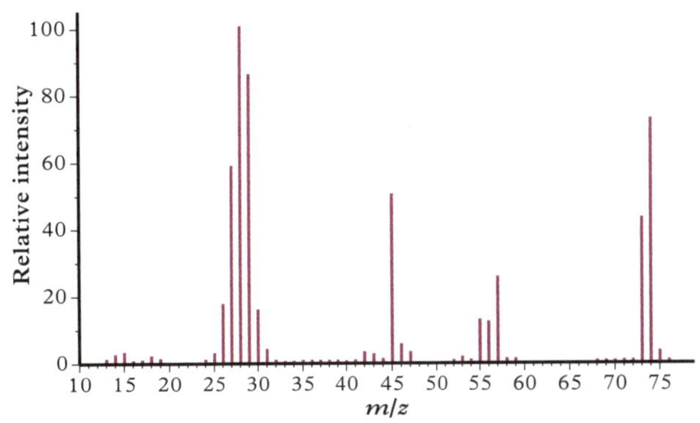

FIGURE 4 Mass spectrum of the compound in Question 7

8 The mass spectrum of the compound in Question 7 is given in Figure 4. **Identify** the species in Table 1, suggesting formulas that correspond to the provided *m*/*z* values.

TABLE 1 *m*/*z* values from the mass spectrum of the compound in Question 7

m/*z* ratio	29	45	73	74
Species				

9 **Deduce** the molecular formula of the compound in Questions 7 and 8.

____

10 In the following diagrams, **select** which arrangement of atoms on the left matches the equivalent x-ray diffraction pattern on the right and connect them using a line.

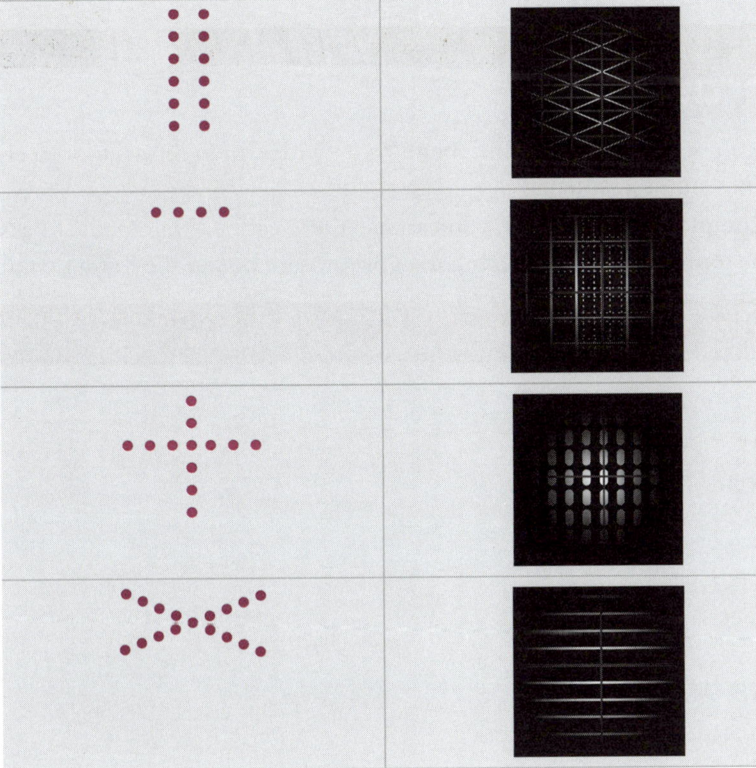

CHAPTER 13

Chemical synthesis

Chemical synthesis forms the basis of many industries, from pharmaceuticals to agriculture. Raw materials are obtained from organic matter, atmospheric gases or the Earth's natural resources. They are purified and converted, under specific conditions, into a range of useful products.

The Haber process, used to produce ammonia, is the combination of nitrogen from the air and hydrogen from natural gas. The contact process, used to produce sulfuric acid, is a three-step process.

Renewable fuels, used to decrease our reliance on fossil fuels, include ethanol, biodiesel and hydrogen. Environmentally friendlier or green chemistry is based on a set of principles that focus on reduction or removal of hazardous waste to ensure manufacturing processes are more cost-effective and energy-efficient, with reduced hazards and waste.

Most fuel cells require hydrogen and oxygen gas input to generate electricity through redox reactions at their electrodes. A phosphoric acid fuel cell generates hydrogen ions and electrons at the anode, then reduces oxygen at the cathode, to generate energy and water.

An alkaline fuel cell oxidises hydrogen at the anode to produce water and electrons, then reduces oxygen at the cathode, to generate energy and water.

Atom economy is a principle of green chemistry and is the theoretical efficiency of a chemical reaction. Theoretical yield is the predicted amount of a product, and actual yield is what is formed.

CHAPTER CHECKLIST

Read this checklist before you complete this chapter's activities, then return to it to check your understanding before your assessments.

Once you have completed this chapter, you can use the 'I can …' statements to assess and rate your understanding of the topics covered by ticking the appropriate box in the 'rating column'.

I can …	Confidently	Partially	Not really
… explain the Haber and contact processes.			
… describe the different biofuels.			
… describe hydrogen fuel cells under different conditions.			
… calculate theoretical yield and percentage yield.			

RESEARCH REVIEW 13

Referencing scientific papers

Chemical synthesis reactions are used to produce paints, inks (Figure 1), cosmetics, explosives, fertilisers, pesticides, soap, detergents, rubber, plastics, packaging, industrial gases, pharmaceuticals, and inorganic and organic chemicals.

FIGURE 1 Most paints, and the plastic containers holding them, are made of synthetic chemicals.

1 **Select** one of the products mentioned above and **identify** three resources on the use of chemical synthesis. Provide both the in-text citation and full reference (for a reference list) for each resource.

Note: Refer back to Research review 2 for guidance on correct referencing techniques.

Resource 1

In-text citation:

____

Full reference:

____

____

____

____

Resource 2

In-text citation:

____

Full reference:

____

____

____

____

Resource 3

In-text citation:

____

Full reference:

____

____

____

EXAM EXCELLENCE 13

Multiple choice – circle the correct answer

1 Energy released in chemical reactions is directly converted to electrical energy in:

A Solar cells

B Electrolytic cells

C Fossil-fuel power stations

D Hydrogen–oxygen fuel cells.

2 The Haber process reaction to produce ammonia can be written as:

$$N_2(g) + 3H_2(g) \rightarrow 2NH_3(g)$$

The mass of ammonia (in tonnes) that could be theoretically produced from 2.0 tonnes of hydrogen gas in an excess of nitrogen gas is closest to:

A 2.0

B 11.4

C 17.1

D 22.8

3 Which of the following is **not** a renewable fuel?

A Biodioesel

B Ethanol

C Hydrogen

D Methane

4 A key reaction in the contact process is the conversion of sulfur dioxide to sulfur trioxide:

$$2SO_2(g) + O_2(g) \rightarrow 2SO_3(g)$$

The maximum amount of sulfur trioxide (in litres) that can be prepared from 100 L of SO_2 and 100 L of O_2, if all gases are at the same temperature and pressure, is:

A 50

B 100

C 150

D 200

5 Biofuels can be sourced by:

A fermenting the sugar components of starch crops

B removing hydrocarbons from the seafloor

C extracting gas from rock reservoirs

D purification of bore water reservoirs.

Short answer

6 Car manufacturers use hydrogen gas as the main fuel in car fuel cells (Figure 2).

This fuel cell has two sections: hydrogen gas is pumped through one half and oxygen gas through the other. The two halves are joined and an alkaline electrolyte passes through the middle. The electrodes consist of a porous nickel alloy mesh.

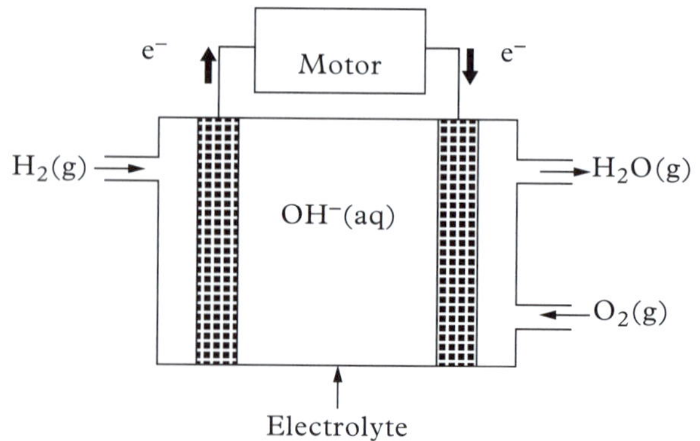

FIGURE 2 A fuel cell

a **Construct** the balanced half-equations for the reactions occurring at the anode and the cathode, including the states.

____

____

b **Deduce** two roles of the nickel alloy electrodes.

____

____

7 Calcium oxide reacts with water at room temperature to form calcium hydroxide.

a **Construct** the balanced chemical equation for this reaction, including the states.

____

b The reaction yields 8 g of an expected 27 g. **Calculate** the percentage yield.

8 A student wanted to produce aluminium iodide in the laboratory by reacting 2.5 g of aluminium metal with 5.0 g of solid iodine.

a **Construct** the balanced chemical equation for this reaction, including the states.

____

b **Calculate** the theoretical mass of aluminium iodide that would be produced by the student in this reaction.

9 One method of making ammonia is shown below as the skeleton equation. **Construct** the balanced equation for this method by adding numbers in front of the different molecules.

Calcium oxide + ammonium chloride → calcium chloride + water + ammonia

$$CaO(s) + NH_4Cl(s) \rightarrow CaCl_2(s) + H_2O(l) + NH_3(g)$$

10 Ethanol is produced in industry by the reaction of ethene with steam, according to the following equation and reaction conditions:

$$CH_2CH_2(g) + H_2O(g) \rightleftharpoons CH_3CH_2OH(g) \qquad \Delta H = -45 \text{ kJ mol}^{-1}$$

Reaction conditions: Temperature = 300°C; Pressure = 60–70 atm; Catalyst = phosphoric(V) acid

A compromise is required for choosing the best temperature for this reaction. **Deduce** a reason for this and **propose** how this will be resolved.

____

____

____

CHAPTER 14

Green chemistry

Environmentally safe or green chemistry is based on a set of 12 principles that focus on reduction or removal of hazardous waste so that the manufacturing process is cost-effective, energy-efficient, hazard-free and waste-free. Use of supercritical fluids or surfactants to replace solvents; use of catalysts to run reactions at lower temperatures; microwave irradiation; photochemistry; sonochemistry; and development and use of biodegradable polymers are examples of the green chemistry principles in action.

Some biochemical fuels can be derived from algae.

Atom economy is an accounting approach for tracking all atoms involved in a reaction, including waste products and side reactions.

For a reaction (excluding any catalysts) of the form

$$aA + bB \rightarrow pP + dD:$$

$$\%\text{ Atom economy} = \frac{(p \times \text{molar mass of P})}{(a \times \text{molar mass of A} + b \times \text{molar mass of B})} \times 100\%$$

where A and B are reactants, P is the desired product and D is a side product. Multi-step reactions can be combined to form an overall reaction prior to calculating the atom economy. A high atom economy of a reaction usually equates to a greener process.

CHAPTER CHECKLIST

Read this checklist before you complete this chapter's activities, then return to it to check your understanding before your assessments.

Once you have completed this chapter, you can use the 'I can …' statements to assess and rate your understanding of the topics covered by ticking the appropriate box in the 'rating column'.

I can …	Confidently	Partially	Not really
… identify and describe the principles of green chemistry.			
… calculate atom economy.			

RESEARCH REVIEW 14

Displaying scientific data graphically

When presenting your research for your internal assessment, it is important to display scientific data correctly.

Below is a graph of how the introduction of the dung beetle to a farm in Western Australia decreased the number of flies. Dung beetles break down cow faeces, which decreases the number of flies. This is an example of a biological alternative to controlling pests. A small site on the farm was investigated for the number of dung beetles and flies from 2010 to 2018.

1 **Identify** the missing features of the graph and annotate them. **Summarise** the results of the graph in a paragraph below.

EXAM EXCELLENCE 14

Multiple choice – circle the correct answer

1 Deduce which of the following is **not** compatible with the principles of green chemistry.

A Maximising energy use in each process

B Minimising the use of toxic chemicals by replacing them with safer alternatives

C Maximising the atom efficiency of each reaction pathway

D Minimising the formation of wastes and by-products.

2 What catalyst increases the reaction time for the hydrolysis of benzamine?

A Microwave heating

B Proteins

C Ice

D No catalyst increases reaction time

3 In green chemistry, the atom economy includes:

A using synthetic pathways that incorporate a maximum proportion of the reactant atoms in the product.

B minimising the energy required for a synthetic pathway so that it is more economical.

C using catalysts that produce only the desired products and prevent formation of other by-products in a synthetic pathway.

D producing a product that is either biodegradable or recycled at the end of its useful lifespan.

4 Which of the following is **not** an example of a biodegradable polymer?

A Polylactic acid

B Polycarprolactone

C Polyvinyl chloride

D Poly-3-hydroxybutanoate

5 Ethanol can be produced by the following synthetic pathway:

$$CH_3CH_2Br(aq) + NaOH(aq) \rightarrow CH_3CH_2OH(aq) + NaBr(aq)$$

Use the principles of green chemistry and atom economy to identify which atoms are considered as waste for this synthetic pathway.

A Sodium and bromine

B Sodium, hydrogen and oxygen

C Carbon, hydrogen and oxygen

D Carbon, hydrogen and bromine

Short answer

6 **Explain** what is meant by the term 'atom economy'.

7 **Calculate** the atom economy for making hydrogen by reacting coal with steam, by constructing the balanced equation for the reaction.

8 A method for capturing solar energy is through its conversion to biomass and biofuels. **Define** the term 'biomass'.

9 **Construct** the equation for percentage yield.

10 Oxygen gas can be produced by two processes as given by the following skeleton equations:
Water electrolysis: $H_2O(l) \rightarrow H_2(g) + O_2(g)$
Decomposition of hydrogen peroxide: $H_2O_2(l) \rightarrow H_2O(l) + O_2(g)$
Calculate the atom economy for each process.

CHAPTER 15 Macromolecules: polymers, proteins and carbohydrates

Polymers are durable, lightweight, non-reactive and occur in nature or can be synthesised or designed for specific purposes. However, the lack of biodegradability of synthetic polymers is an ongoing environmental concern, which is partially being addressed with recycling codes on polymer products. Polymers produced by addition polymerisation are formed from alkenes in addition reactions. Polymers produced by condensation polymerisation are formed from reagents with two functional groups that react together and lose a small molecule.

Proteins are structurally similar to each other and are synthesised from 20 different α-amino acids. Each α-amino acid consists of an amino functional group and a carboxylic acid group both attached to a carbon atom. Proteins are polymers built from amino acid monomers by condensation reactions. This process forms an amide/peptide linkage between the amino group of one amino acid and the carboxylic acid group of the next.

The long polypeptide chains formed from multiple amino acid monomers can form primary, secondary, and tertiary and quaternary structures. Carbohydrates are a broad group of macromolecules that are classified as monosaccharides, disaccharides or polysaccharides.

Monosaccharides join together to form disaccharides through a condensation reaction. This reaction requires very specific enzymes, depending on the substrate or molecule(s) to be acted on by the enzyme. During this condensation reaction, a water molecule is lost; hence the formula for a disaccharide is $C_{12}H_{22}O_{11}$.

CHAPTER CHECKLIST

Read this checklist before you complete this chapter's activities, then return to it to check your understanding before your assessments.

Once you have completed this chapter, you can use the 'I can …' statements to assess and rate your understanding of the topics covered by ticking the appropriate box in the 'rating column'.

I can …	Confidently	Partially	Not really
… identify the different addition and condensation polymers.			
… explain the different uses of polymers.			
... describe amino acids and polypeptides.			
… understand the formation of monosaccharides, disaccharides and polysaccharides.			

RESEARCH REVIEW 15

Reading an abstract

The following abstract discusses natural polymers being used in tumour therapy.

> Chitin and chitosan are natural polysaccharide polymers. These polymers have been used in several agricultural, food protection and nutraceutical applications. Moreover, chitin and chitosan have been also used in biomedical and biotechnological applications as drug delivery systems or in pharmaceutical formulations. So far, there are only few studies dealing with arsenic (As) removal from groundwater using chitin or chitosan and no evidence of the use of these natural polymers for arsenic trioxide (As_2O_3) delivery in tumor therapy. Here we suggest that chitin and/or chitosan might have the right properties to be employed as efficient polymers for such applications. Besides, nanotechnology offers suitable tools for the fabrication of novel nanostructured materials of natural origin. Since different nanostructured materials have already been employed successfully in various multidisciplinary fields, we expect that the integration of nanotechnology and natural polymer chemistry will further lead to innovative applications for environment and medicine.

1 **Identify** the gap in the scientific knowledge that has initiated this study.

____

____

____

____

____

2 **Summarise** the main results of this study.

____

____

____

____

____

____

____

3 **Use** the digital object identifier (DOI) for this abstract to search for and then reference the article as a full reference (as in a reference list).
The DOI can be copied directly into Google Scholar: DOI: 10.3390/md8051518

____

____

____

____

____

____

EXAM EXCELLENCE 15

Multiple choice – circle the correct answer

1 Identify the reaction that describes the polymerisation of glucose to form cellulose.

A Addition

B Hydrolysis

C Substitution

D Condensation.

2 Select which one of the following polymers that is **not** an addition polymer.

A Polypropene

B Polyamide

C Polystyrene

D Polyvinyl chloride.

3 Identify which molecule is a carbohydrate:

A CH_4

B $C_{16}H_{32}O_{16}$

C $C_{18}H_{34}O_2$

D $C_3H_7NO_2$

4 Deduce the purpose of the bond between the cysteine (Cys) molecules in the ox insulin structure in Figure 1.

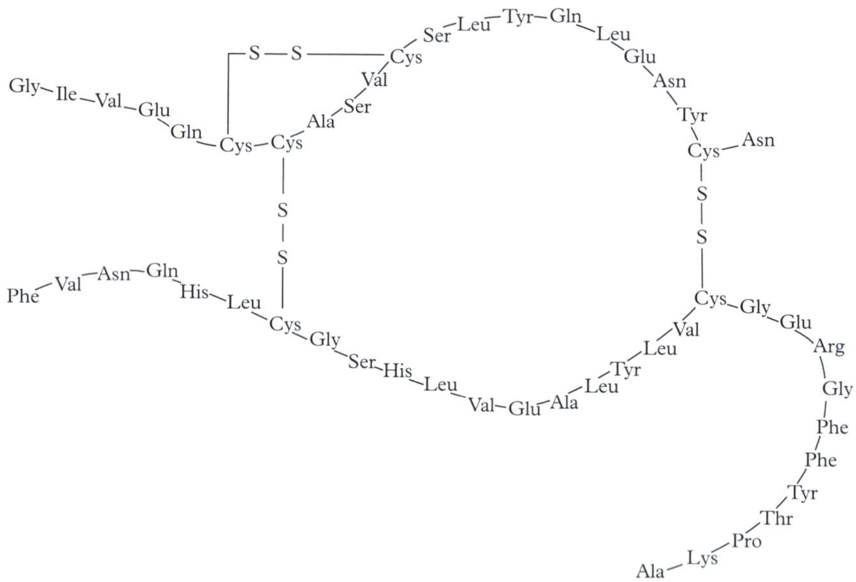

FIGURE 1 Primary structure of ox insulin

A To support the primary structure of a protein

B To support the secondary structure of a protein

C To support the tertiary structure of a protein

D To support the primary, secondary and tertiary structures of a protein

5 If the empirical formula of an amino acid is C_3H_7NO, select the correct name from the following options.

A Valine

B Lysine

C Aspartic acid

D Leucine

Short answer

6 A section of an addition polymer is shown in Figure 2. **Sketch** the monomer used to produce this polymer.

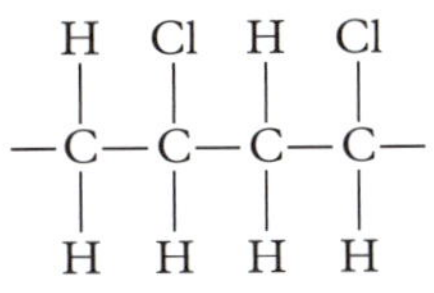

```
 H  Cl  H  Cl
 |   |   |   |
—C—C—C—C—
 |   |   |   |
 H   H   H   H
```

FIGURE 2 A section of an addition polymer

7 Flowers produce nectar, which is a mixture of sugars, such as glucose and sucrose. **Identify** which group of compounds that glucose belongs to.

____

8 **Sketch** the structure of the amino acid proline existing at a pH of 2.

9 **a** Ethene is an example of an unsaturated hydrocarbon. **Define** the term 'unsaturated'.

____

____

____

b **Sketch** the structural formula (with correct shape) of ethene.

10 The structure of a dipeptide is shown in Figure 3. **Sketch** a circle on the structure to the right to show the dipeptide link.

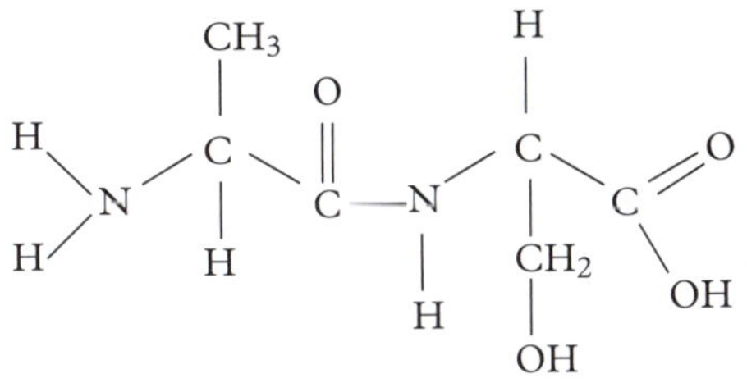

$H_2N–CH(CH_3)–C(=O)–NH–CH(CH_2OH)–C(=O)OH$

FIGURE 3 The structure of a dipeptide

Molecular manufacturing

Nanomolecular science is the study of the behaviour of objects at a very small scale, roughly 1 to 100 nanometres (nm). Nanomolecular-sized particles have very high surface-area-to-volume ratios, which impart them with different physical and chemical properties compared with those of macro- or larger-sized particles, including different optical, mechanical, electrical and thermal properties.

Nanomolecular manufacturing is the precise placement of an arrangement of atoms or molecules, in order to build larger molecular assemblies or molecular-based machines. Three types of processes include bottom-up, top-down and self-assembly. Most of the self-assembly processes occur naturally, like the use of bacteria to oxidise ethanol to make vinegar, ribosomes and enzymes in cellular processes, ion pumps to transport neurotransmitters, kinesin to transport proteins and the photosynthetic machinery in chloroplasts. The use of scanning tunnelling and atomic force microscopy enables the processes of bottom-up, the building up of nanomolecular structures atom by atom, and top-down, using small-scale versions of machines to cut and shape structures into nanomolecular-sized pieces.

Early molecular machines included the mechanically interlocked molecular systems of rotaxanes, catenanes and molecular knots, and the nanomolecular chemical sensors used to measure the amount of glucose in blood.

Eric Drexler proposed three types of nanomolecular machines (assemblers, disassemblers and self-replicators) and envisaged wider acceptance of this technology to recycle or eliminate existing waste. Sceptics believed that more and uncontrolled self-replicating nanomolecular machines would turn everything into a 'grey goo'. Scientists are hopeful that in the future, (the now hypothetical) nanorobots will be so advanced to mimic natural biological processes to streamline and improve pharmaceutical and other medical treatments.

CHAPTER CHECKLIST

Read this checklist before you complete this chapter's activities, then return to it to check your understanding before your assessments.

Once you have completed this chapter, you can use the 'I can …' statements to assess and rate your understanding of the topics covered by ticking the appropriate box in the 'rating column'.

I can …	Confidently	Partially	Not really
… describe what nanomachines are.			
… explain the development of molecular manufacturing.			

RESEARCH REVIEW 16

Writing a research question

The following claim was suggested about nanomolecular manufacturing processes:

Nanomolecular manufacturing processes are time-consuming, a health and safety hazard and, if left uncontrolled, the resultant products will all be a 'grey goo'.

1 **Create** a research question(s) for this claim.

2 Because molecular manufacturing is a new area of chemistry, it can be difficult to find credible resources of information. **Investigate** nanomolecular manufacturing and **critique** the credibility of resources on this topic.

3 **Identify** three issues in finding credible resources.

EXAM EXCELLENCE 16

Multiple choice – circle the correct answer

1 Nanomolecular particles have different physical and chemical properties compared with those of macro- or larger-sized particles of the same substance. This is because the nanomolecular particles have:

A a decreased atomic mass

B a higher solubility

C a greater surface-area-to-volume ratio

D a greater ratio of protons to electrons.

2 The prefix 'nano' is defined as:

A 1×10^{-3}

B 1×10^{-9}

C 1×10^{-6}

D 1×10^{-12}

3 Roxanes are:

A an assembly of molecules containing two or more mechanically interlocking rings.

B an assembly of molecular components, including a dumbbell-shaped molecule.

C molecular systems with defined energy input that can perform a useful function at the nanoscale.

D chemical sensors used widely in medicine.

4 Nanorobots in biomedical applications contrast with nanomolecular-manufactured chemical sensors because:

A they do not exist yet.

B they exist in an experimental form in laboratories.

C they are already in use for biomedical, forensic and toxicology applications.

D they contain mechanical components that detect and measure molecules in biological fluids.

5 The 'smart' contact lens is an example of a:

A nanotube

B nanorobot

C biological molecular machine

D chemical sensor.

Short answer

6 Convert the following lengths into nanometres. **Apply** correct scientific notation.

a 5 cm

b 12 mm

c 2 km

7 **Describe** and **explain** two properties of macro- or larger-sized particles of a substance compared with those of nanomolecular-sized particles of the same substance.

8 **Describe** and **explain** the three types of nanomolecular manufacturing processes.

9 **Critique** and **summarise** how the scanning tunnelling microscope (STM) can be used to view nanomolecular structures.

10 Catalysts are substances that increase the rate of a reaction without being consumed themselves, and they operate by adsorbing reactants onto their surface.

Describe and **explain** how a catalyst comprising of nanomolecular-sized particles would be more effective than a macro- or larger-sized particle catalyst.

UNIT 4

PRACTICE ASSESSMENT

Structure, synthesis and design

Throughout the chapters you have practised analysing and recording data, conducting research and modifying experiments.

In this section, you will complete the following internal assessment:

- the Research investigation (20%).

Note: The assessment provided here is a practice assessment. The final structure of the internal assessment will be set by the QCAA.

Unit 4 Research investigation

CASE STUDY

Biochemical fuels: will they replace fossil fuels?

Most of our energy needs are met by burning fossil fuels such as coal and crude oil (petroleum and natural gas). Coal is used to generate electricity, and petroleum is used as a transport fuel. Other products derived from crude oil are used to make plastics and pharmaceuticals. There are large reserves of coal; however, petroleum deposits are limited. The known oil reserves found have decreased, while the demand for oil has increased due to the increasing world population. This situation provides motivation to devise new renewable and sustainable energy sources.

Biochemical fuels can be derived from plant material (Figure 1), such as grains (maize, wheat and barley) and sugar cane, or vegetable wastes and vegetable oils. Biochemical fuels can be either used alone or blended with fossil fuels such as petrol and diesel.

The plant materials used in the generation of biochemical fuels are produced by photosynthesis, which removes carbon dioxide (CO_2) from the atmosphere. Biochemical fuels are thought to not increase atmospheric CO_2. Although CO_2 is released back into the atmosphere when the biochemical fuel is burnt, CO_2 is also removed during the process of photosynthesis. Hence, biochemical fuels are said to be 'carbon dioxide neutral'.

Arguments for the development of biochemical fuels include: their use will reduce CO_2 emissions and reduce the greenhouse effect; the land use for the production of biofuel utilises waste materials remaining from food production; and biochemical fuel production uses resources that are available in Australia, decreasing the need for importing raw materials and providing sustainable employment.

However, the major argument against the production of biochemical fuels is that the land use will detract from providing food crops.

FIGURE 1 Biochemical fuels can be derived from plant material.

Your task is to conduct a Research investigation about the following claim, which is related to the case study above:

Biochemical fuels are a renewable energy source that can directly reduce our dependence on liquid fossil fuels.

Research question

Research

Note: This section provides space for you to investigate two sources; you will need to research further to complete the assessment.

Resource 1

- Title:
- Author(s):
- Source and credibility:
- Publication date:
- Aim:
- Resource's research question:
- Methodology
  - What data was collected?
  - How was the data collected?
- Results
  - Did the resource support your research question?
  - Why does/doesn't it support the provided claim?

Resource 2

- Title:
- Author(s):
- Source and credibility:
- Publication date:
- Aim:
- Resource's research question:
- Methodology
  - What data was collected?
  - How was the data collected?
- Results
  - Did the resource support your research question?
  - Why does/doesn't it support the provided claim?

Planning your internal assessment

Practical manual

The QCAA Chemistry General Senior Syllabus outlines a number of mandatory and suggested practicals for completion in Units 3 & 4. All practicals are included in this chapter.

Suggestions for methodology and materials have been supplied in this chapter. However, the following is not prescriptive; schools may complete mandatory or suggested practicals in any other form suited to their resources.

The experiments in this chapter have been trialled and cautions of obvious hazards given; however, it is the legal obligation of the individual teacher to carry out their own risk assessment prior to undertaking any practical activity.

If you are unsure of any procedures in the lab or need any clarification for a practical, consult your teacher and/or lab technician.

⚠ SAFETY

This chapter will highlight key safety concerns within each practical; however, there are some general safety concerns to be considered before completing all practicals.

- Hair should be tied back.
- Do not eat or drink in the lab.
- Always be aware of your peers and act sensibly.
- Wear a lab coat, safety glasses, closed-toed shoes and gloves.
- Review the school's safety procedures and location of eye wash, shower, spill kits and first aid kits.
- Handle all chemicals with care and consult your teacher and risk assessments for the hazards involved with each chemical.
- Keep open flames away from flammable materials.
- Handle hot materials with the appropriate equipment (i.e. heat-resistant gloves or tongs).
- Always check that electrical equipment have no damaged or exposed wires before use.

2.2A SUGGESTED PRACTICAL Effect of concentration on equilibrium

CAUTION: ALL CHEMICALS ARE IRRITANTS. NaF IS TOXIC IF SWALLOWED. $Fe(NO_3)_3$ IS AN IRRITANT. $AgNO_3$ IS TOXIC AND CAN LEAVE BLACK/GREY STAINS ON THE SKIN. WEAR PERSONAL PROTECTIVE EQUIPMENT AT ALL TIMES. IF THE CHEMICALS COME IN CONTACT WITH SKIN, FLUSH THE AFFECTED AREA FOR 15 MINUTES, AND CONSULT A HEALTHCARE PROFESSIONAL IF ANY CHEMICALS ARE INGESTED. CONSULT YOUR LAB TECHNICIAN WHEN DISPOSING OF THE CHEMICALS.

Unit 3, Topic 1: Investigate Le Châtelier's principle.

Source: *Chemistry 2019 v1.3 General Senior Syllabus* © Queensland Curriculum & Assessment Authority

Context

This experiment is based on the iron(III) thiocyanate equilibrium system:

$$Fe^{3+}(aq) + SCN^{-}(aq) \rightleftharpoons FeSCN^{2+}(aq) \quad \Delta H = \text{exothermic}$$

yellow colourless red

The initial equilibrium mixture should be orange in colour because it is a mixture of the yellow and red colours. As reactants or products are added or removed, the system will partially oppose the change and move to one side of the reaction in a net forward or reverse direction. A net forward reaction will cause the system to become more red or darker, and a net reverse reaction will cause the system to become more yellow or lighter.

Aim

To determine the effect that an increase or decrease in concentration has on the position of an equilibrium reaction.

Materials

- 30 mL 0.005 M $FeSCN^{2+}$ solution (a mixture of $Fe(NO_3)_3$ and KSCN in a dropper bottle)
- 0.1 M $Fe(NO_3)_3$ in a dropper bottle
- 0.1 M KSCN in a dropper bottle
- 0.1 M NaF in a dropper bottle
- 0.1 M $AgNO_3$ in a dropper bottle
- Wash bottle with deionised water
- 5 × micro test tubes
- Pen for labelling glassware
- Micro test-tube rack

Method

1 Label the five test tubes as 'A', 'B', 'C', 'D' and 'E' and place them in the test-tube rack.

2 Add the $FeSCN^{2+}$ solution to all test tubes so that they are one-third full. Record the initial colour of the solution in the test tubes in Table 1.

3 Add solutions to each test tube as follows:
   - A: Add one drop of $Fe(NO_3)_3$.
   - B: Add one drop of KSCN.
   - C: Add one drop of NaF.
   - D: Add one drop of $AgNO_3$.
   - E: Add an equal volume of deionised water (total volume of the test tube should be two-thirds full).

4 Record the colour changes of each test tube in Table 1. **Note:** If the Fe^{3+} is pale yellow and the $FeSCN^{2+}$ is red, the colour changes should be lighter/yellow, darker/red or no change.

Results

Record your results in Table 1 below.

TABLE 1 Colour changes for each of the test tubes

Test tube	Test	Initial colour	Final colour
A	Add $Fe(NO_3)_3$		
B	Add KSCN		
C	Add NaF		
D	Add $AgNO_3$		
E	Add an equal volume of deionised water		

Discussion

1 For each test, state how the addition of each substance changes the concentration of the reaction system (e.g. lowers the concentration of $FeSCN^{2+}$) and whether a net forward or reverse reaction results, based on the data you have gathered.

2 Using the short-answer structure, use Le Châtelier's principle to explain the colour changes that occur in each test tube. Your answer must reference exothermic/endothermic, energy, a partial opposition to a change, and a net forward or reverse reaction to release or store energy from the bonds of the reactants or products.

3 Draw a graph for each test tube which represents the initial equilibrium, the change that occurs and the new equilibrium. **Note:** This graph will illustrate the general change because no concentration numbers are able to be determined.

4 State the equilibrium expression for the reaction.

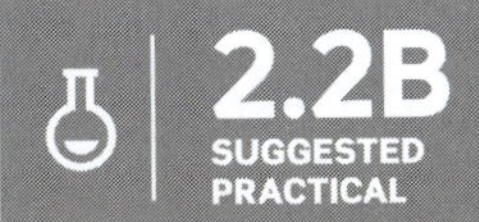

Effect of volume and pressure on equilibrium

CAUTION: TEACHER-ONLY DEMONSTRATION! ALL CHEMICALS ARE IRRITANTS. NO_2/N_2O_4 GAS IS HIGHLY TOXIC AND CAN CAUSE BURNS AND SERIOUS RISK TO EYES. IF THE CHEMICALS COME IN CONTACT WITH SKIN, FLUSH THE AFFECTED AREA FOR 15 MINUTES AND CONSULT A HEALTHCARE PROFESSIONAL. WEAR PERSONAL PROTECTIVE EQUIPMENT AT ALL TIMES AND COMPLETE THE EXPERIMENT IN A FUME CUPBOARD. NO CHEMICALS ARE TO BE HANDLED BY STUDENTS.

Unit 3, Topic 1: Investigate factors that affect equilibrium. Simulations could be used.

Source: *Chemistry 2019 v1.3 General Senior Syllabus* © Queensland Curriculum & Assessment Authority

Context

A mixture of gases, N_2O_4 and NO_2, are contained within a syringe. The N_2O_4 is colourless, whereas the NO_2 is a dark brown colour.

$$N_2O_4(g) \rightleftharpoons 2NO_2(g) \quad \Delta H = \text{endothermic}$$

Aim

To determine the effect that an increase or decrease in volume or pressure has on the position of an equilibrium reaction.

Materials

- NO_2/N_2O_4 gas mixture
- Large gas syringe
- Rubber stopper for the nozzle of the syringe: ensure it is properly sealed and no gas can escape

Method

1. Ensure that the plunger is situated so that it can be both pulled out and pushed in without any gas escaping.
2. While in the fume cupboard, hold the syringe and ask students to record the colour.
3. While holding the sealed end of the syringe (to ensure there are no leaks), press the plunger inwards to compress the gas and hold it in for at least 5 seconds. Students must record the initial colour change (when the plunger went in) and the final colour change that happens after that.
4. Again holding the sealed end of the syringe (to ensure there are no leaks), pull the plunger outwards to reduce the pressure of the gas and hold it there for at least 5 seconds. Students must record the initial colour change (when the plunger was pulled out) and the final colour change that happens after that.

Results

Initial colour of the gas mixture:

____

____

____

____

Record the results in Table 1 below by stating 'lighter' or 'darker'.

TABLE 1 Colour changes for each of the experiments

Change in volume	Initial colour change	Final colour change
Decrease		
Increase		

Discussion

1 Explain why two colour changes occur when the volume of the system is changed.

2 Explain the colour changes that occur when there is an increase in volume, by referencing Le Châtelier's principle.

3 Explain the colour changes that occur when there is a decrease in volume, by referencing Le Châtelier's principle.

4 In a separate reaction, colourless hydrogen gas and dark-purple iodine gas are reacted to form colourless hydrogen iodide gas, according to the following equation:

$$H_2(g) + I_2(g) \rightleftharpoons 2HI(g)$$

a Explain the colour changes that occur when there is an increase in volume, by referencing Le Châtelier's principle.

b Explain the colour changes that occur when there is a decrease in volume, by referencing Le Châtelier's principle.

2.2C SUGGESTED PRACTICAL

Effect of temperature on equilibrium

CAUTION: TEACHER-ONLY DEMONSTRATION! ALL CHEMICALS ARE IRRITANTS. NO_2/N_2O_4 GAS IS HIGHLY TOXIC AND CAN CAUSE BURNS AND SERIOUS RISK TO EYES. METHYL VIOLET INDICATOR AND H_3PO_4 ARE IRRITANTS. IF THE CHEMICALS COME IN CONTACT WITH SKIN, FLUSH THE AFFECTED AREA FOR 15 MINUTES AND CONSULT A HEALTHCARE PROFESSIONAL. WEAR PERSONAL PROTECTIVE EQUIPMENT AT ALL TIMES AND COMPLETE THE EXPERIMENT IN A FUME CUPBOARD. NO CHEMICALS ARE TO BE HANDLED BY STUDENTS.

Unit 3, Topic 1: Investigate reversible reactions.

Source: *Chemistry 2019 v1.3 General Senior Syllabus* © Queensland Curriculum & Assessment Authority

Context

Three equilibrium systems will be analysed in this experiment.

$$Fe^{3+}(aq) + SCN^{-}(aq) \rightleftharpoons FeSCN^{2+}(aq) \quad \Delta H = \text{exothermic}$$

Iron(III) is yellow in colour, and iron thiocyanate is dark red in colour.

$$H_3PO_4(aq) \rightleftharpoons H_2PO_4^{-}(aq) + H^{+}(aq) \quad \Delta H = \text{exothermic}$$

Using methyl violet indicator, an increase in hydronium concentration results in a yellow colour. A lower hydronium concentration results in a green/blue colour.

$$N_2O_4(g) \rightleftharpoons 2NO_2(g) \quad \Delta H = \text{endothermic}$$

N_2O_4 is a colourless gas, whereas NO_2 is a dark-brown gas.

Aim

To determine the effect of increasing and decreasing the temperature in an exothermic and endothermic system on the position of equilibrium.

Materials

- 30 mL 0.005 M $FeSCN^{2+}$ solution (a mixture of $Fe(NO_3)_3$ and KSCN in a dropper bottle)
- 30 mL 1 M phosphoric acid (H_3PO_4)
- Methyl violet indicator
- 3 × stoppered test tubes filled with a mixture of NO_2/N_2O_4 gases
- 6 × test tubes
- 3 × 250 mL beakers (one empty, one half-filled with ice water and one half-filled with hot water from a kettle)
- Kettle
- Ice
- Heatproof mat
- Test-tube rack

Method

1 Prepare the three 250 mL beakers so that one is empty (this will be the room temperature beaker), one is half-filled with iced water and one is half-filled with hot water.

2 Add the $FeSCN^{2+}$ solution to three of the test tubes until they are one-third full and place them in the test-tube rack.

3 Add two drops of methyl violet indicator to the other three test tubes and then add the H_3PO_4 solution until they are one-third full. **Note:** If the methyl violet is placed on top of the H_3PO_4 solution, it can be hard to mix. Add the methyl violet first.

4 Place one $FeSCN^{2+}$ test tube and one H_3PO_4 test tube into the room-temperature beaker, one $FeSCN^{2+}$ test tube and one H_3PO_4 test tube into the iced-water beaker, and one $FeSCN^{2+}$ test tube and one H_3PO_4 test tube into the hot-water beaker.
5 Record the results of each solution at room temperature, cold and hot in Table 1.
6 Remove the test tubes from the beakers and place them in the test-tube rack. Take the three beakers to the fume cupboard where the stoppered test tubes filled with a mixture of NO_2/N_2O_4 gases must be tested.
7 Place one of each of the test tubes into each beaker in the fume cupboard and leave them for a couple of minutes. Record the changes in Table 1.

Results

Record the results in Table 1.

TABLE 1 Colour changes for each of the experiments

Test	Colour of the substance in the test tube		
	Hot	Room temperature	Cold
$FeSCN^{2+}$ solution			
H_3PO_4 solution			
NO_2/N_2O_4 gases			

Discussion

1 For each test, use the results to explain whether the addition of heat will cause a net forward or net reverse reaction.

____

____

____

____

____

____

2 For each test, use the results to explain whether the removal of heat will cause a net forward or net reverse reaction.

____

____

____

____

____

3 Using the short-answer structure, use Le Châtelier's principle to explain the colour changes that occur in each test tube. Your answer must reference exothermic/endothermic, energy, a partial opposition to a change, and a net forward or reverse reaction to release or store energy from the bonds of the reactants or products.

4 Draw a graph for each hot and cold test tube that represents the initial equilibrium, the change that occurs and the new equilibrium. **Note:** These graphs will illustrate the general change because no concentration numbers are able to be determined.

5 Write the equilibrium expression for each of the reactions.

Measuring pH

Unit 3, Topic 1: Measure pH of a substance.

Source: *Chemistry 2019 v1.3 General Senior Syllabus* © Queensland Curriculum & Assessment Authority

Aim

To identify the pH level of different substances by using pH indicators, pH test papers and a pH meter.

Materials

- pH indicators (e.g. methyl orange, methyl red etc.)
- Universal indicator
- Litmus paper (blue or red)
- pH meter
- Vinegar
- Milk
- Lemon juice
- Bleach
- Lemonade
- Shampoo
- Deionised water
- Beakers

Method

1 Pour each liquid into a separate beaker.

2 Measure the pH of each liquid with all of the available pH indicators.

3 Record your observations and measurements in Table 1 below.

Results

Record your results in Table 1.

TABLE 1 pH measurements of different substances

Substance	Observations and pH measurements				
	Methyl red	Litmus paper (blue)	Litmus paper (red)	Universal indicator	pH meter
Vinegar					
Milk					
Lemon juice					

Substance	Observations and pH measurements				
	Methyl red	Litmus paper (blue)	Litmus paper (red)	Universal indicator	pH meter
Bleach					
Lemonade					
Shampoo					
Deionised water					

Discussion

1 Discuss and compare all your measurements.

2 What pH measurement is the most accurate/reliable and why?

3 What could be different applications for the different pH indicators?

4 Discuss the validity of your data.

4.1 SUGGESTED PRACTICAL

Electrical conductivity of strong and weak acids and bases

CAUTION: ALL CHEMICALS ARE IRRITANTS. HCl IS AN IRRITANT AND CORROSIVE. SODIUM HYDROXIDE IS CORROSIVE AND AN IRRITANT. WEAR PERSONAL PROTECTIVE EQUIPMENT AT ALL TIMES. IF THE CHEMICALS COME IN CONTACT WITH SKIN, FLUSH THE AFFECTED AREA FOR 15 MINUTES AND CONSULT A HEALTHCARE PROFESSIONAL. DAMAGED OR EXPOSED WIRES CAN CAUSE SHOCKS. HANDLE WITH CARE.

Unit 3, Topic 1: Investigate the electrical conductivity of strong and weak acids and bases (simulation can be used).

Source: *Chemistry 2019 v1.3 General Senior Syllabus* © Queensland Curriculum & Assessment Authority

Aim

To investigate the different degrees of electrical conductivity of strong and weak acids and bases.

Materials

- 1 light emitting diode (LED)
- 1 kΩ resistor
- 1 × 9 V battery
- 3 pieces of wire
- 100 mL 1 M solution of acetic acid, CH_3COOH (weak acid)
- 100 mL 1 M solution of hydrochloric acid, HCl (strong acid)
- 100 mL 1 M solution of ammonia, NH_3 (weak base)
- 100 mL 1 M solution of sodium hydroxide, $NaOH$ (strong base)

Method

1. Predict which solution will conduct electricity the best, prior to performing the experiment. Record your predictions in Table 1.
2. Construct the light bulb apparatus as shown in Figure 1. Make sure you attach the longer wire of the LED to the resistor. Electricity can only flow one direction through a LED.
3. Measure all solutions by using the apparatus. Make sure you don't touch the exposed wires of the electrodes with your fingers, and keep the wires separated while measuring.

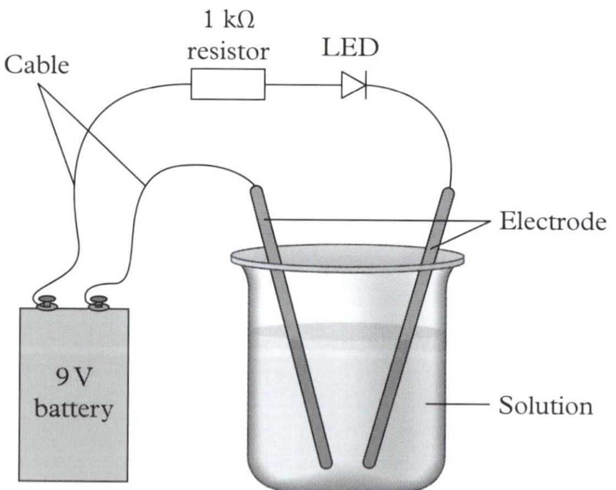

FIGURE 1 A light bulb apparatus that tests the conductivity of solutions

Results

Record your results in Table 1 on the next page.

TABLE 1 Results from conductivity experiments

Solution	Prediction	LED brightness*	Conductivity**
Acetic acid			
Hydrochloric acid			
Ammonia			
Sodium hydroxide			

*Use these descriptors: off, dim, medium, bright, very bright.
**Use these conductivity descriptors: none/low, low, medium, high, very high.

Discussion

1 Do your results agree with your prediction? Why or why not?

____

____

____

2 Discuss why some solutions in the investigation conduct electricity better than others.

____

____

____

____

3 Look up all K_a and K_b values of the used solutions and compare them with your results. Is there a correlation?

____

____

____

____

____

Titration of hydrochloric acid with a standard sodium carbonate solution

CAUTION: ALL CHEMICALS ARE IRRITANTS. HCl IS CORROSIVE. WEAR PERSONAL PROTECTIVE EQUIPMENT AT ALL TIMES. IF THE CHEMICALS COME IN CONTACT WITH SKIN, FLUSH THE AFFECTED AREA FOR 15 MINUTES AND CONSULT A HEALTHCARE PROFESSIONAL.

Unit 3, Topic 1: Acid–base titration to calculate the concentration of a solution with reference to a standard solution.

Source: *Chemistry 2019 v1.3 General Senior Syllabus* © Queensland Curriculum & Assessment Authority

Note: Select Practical 5.1A or Practical 5.1B as the mandatory practical to cover this syllabus point.

Context

Sodium carbonate (Na_2CO_3) is a relatively strong base, which reacts with hydrochloric acid, a strong acid, according to the overall equation:

$$2HCl(aq) + Na_2CO_3(aq) \rightarrow 2NaCl(aq) + H_2O(l) + CO_2(g)$$

This occurs in two steps.

Step 1:

$$Na_2CO_3(aq) + HCl(aq) \rightarrow NaHCO_3(aq) + NaCl(aq)$$

Step 2:

$$NaHCO_3(aq) + HCl(aq) \rightarrow NaCl(aq) + H_2O(l) + CO_2(g)$$

In the first step, one of the sodium ions from the Na_2CO_3 swaps places with the hydrogen ion from the HCl. When the equivalence point is reached in step 1, the product $NaHCO_3$ (sodium bicarbonate (baking soda)) makes the solution basic. As the equivalence point occurs in basic conditions, a phenolphthalein indicator can be used.

In the second step, the bicarbonate reacts with more HCl to form a neutral solution of NaCl, H_2O and CO_2. Methyl orange is a more suitable indicator for this reaction.

As the overall equivalence point occurs at a neutral pH, the methyl orange indicator will be used. Methyl orange changes colour from red at pH 3.1 to yellow at pH 4.4. This is in the equivalence point range of the reaction's titration curve.

Aim

To determine the concentration of a solution of hydrochloric acid by titration against a standard sodium carbonate solution, using a methyl orange indicator.

Materials

Part A

- 2.5 g pure sodium carbonate (Na_2CO_3)
- Deionised water
- 200 mL volumetric flask
- Electronic balance
- Weigh boat
- Spatula
- Funnel (**Important:** Ensure the funnel has been washed with deionised water and allowed to completely air-dry before the experiment.)
- Pen for labelling glassware
- Plastic dropping pipette

Part B

- Standard solution of Na_2CO_3 from Part A
- Hydrochloric acid (HCl) solution (with an approximate concentration of 0.5 M)
- Methyl orange indicator
- 50 mL burette
- Retort stand and burette clamp (if there is no burette clamp, use a boss head and clamp)
- White tile
- 10.00 mL pipette
- Pipette bulb
- 3 × 100 mL beakers
- 250 mL beaker
- 3 × 100 mL conical flasks
- Pen for labelling glassware
- Wash bottle with deionised water

Method

Part A: Preparation of a standard sodium carbonate solution

1 Place a weigh boat on the electronic balance and tare it to read zero.

2 Use a spatula to measure 2.5 g of sodium carbonate into the weigh boat and record its mass. **Note:** This does not need to be exactly 2.5 g, but should be within 0.1 g of 2.5 g.

3 Wash the volumetric flask with deionised water from the wash bottle. Add the lid, shake the flask and then tip the water down the sink. Repeat this two more times.

4 Add a small volume (approximately 20 mL) of deionised water to the volumetric flask. This will help to stop the Na_2CO_3 clumping together and solidifying at the bottom of the flask.

5 Put the prewashed and dried funnel in the mouth of the volumetric flask. Add the Na_2CO_3 to the volumetric flask by scraping it out of the weigh boat a small amount at a time. Ensure that the solid moves through the funnel and into the volumetric flask before adding more solid. Tap the funnel if the solid gets stuck (**do not add water to wash it through** – the Na_2CO_3 will clump together and become very difficult to remove). When nearly all of the solid is in the flask and only a small amount remains in the weigh boat and filter funnel, use the wash bottle to rinse the weigh boat into the funnel.

6 Fill the volumetric flask to one-quarter full and swirl it until all the Na_2CO_3 is dissolved. This may take extra time if the powder clumps together and solidifies but it will dissolve eventually.

7 Add deionised water until the bottom of the meniscus is on the mark (this should be on the neck of the flask).

8 Put the lid on the flask and tip the flask upside down and then upright again. Repeat this motion until the solution has an evenly distributed concentration.

9 Label the flask 'Na_2CO_3', add its concentration, the date it was prepared and your initials.

Part B: Determining the concentration of a hydrochloric acid solution

1 Label three 100 mL beakers as 'washing deionised water', 'HCl' and 'Na_2CO_3' and fill each beaker with its respective solution.

2 Wash three 100 mL conical flasks with deionised water and tip the waste down the sink.

3 Wash the 10 mL pipette by drawing the washing water up to the mark and then dispensing it down the sink. Repeat this step two more times.

4 Using the pipette, dispense 10 mL of the HCl solution into the conical flask. Repeat this step two more times so that all three conical flasks contain a 10 mL aliquot of HCl. Add three drops of methyl orange indicator to each conical flask.

5 Close the stopcock of the burette and wash it with deionised water from the wash bottle by adding some water and gently tipping the burette onto its side, then slowly spinning it to ensure the water has come in contact with the inside of the burette. Empty some of the water into the sink by tipping

the burette upside down; pour the remaining water out the tip by opening the stopcock. Repeat this one more time.

6 Using no more than 10 mL of the standard Na_2CO_3 solution, repeat Step 5. Do not dispose of the solution down the sink. Dispose of it in the waste beaker. This wash only needs to be performed once.

7 Set up the burette and clamp (see Figure 1).

8 Place the 250 mL beaker under the burette (to collect the waste) and a funnel on the top. With the stopcock open, pour in the standard solution until no more than 1–2 mL has run through. Then close the stopcock and fill the burette to the top. (**Note:** The burette does not need to be filled to the 0.00 mL line. A final and initial volume will be measured, so it does not matter what value it starts on, as long as it is below 5 mL.) Remove the funnel from the top. Record the initial volume in the burette.

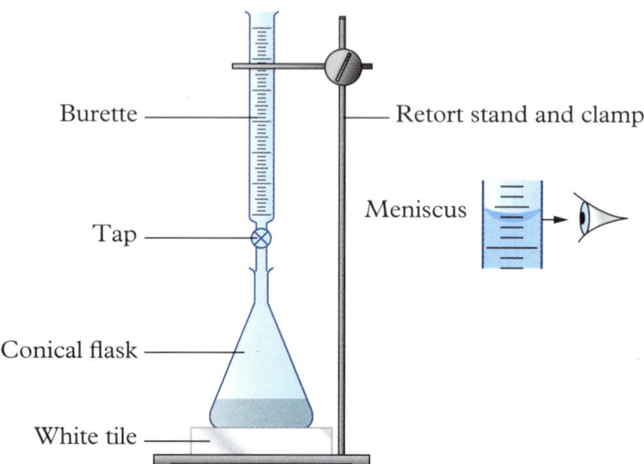

FIGURE 1 The apparatus for the titration

9 Place the first conical flask under the burette and carefully open the stopcock. As the Na_2CO_3 mixes with the HCl solution, red/dark orange will be visible in the flask. Constantly swirl the flask to turn the red to orange. If the solution turns yellow, it has gone too far. This end point can be difficult to observe. Take your time, use the white tile and be careful. Turn the stopcock so that the Na_2CO_3 solution is dispensed at a slower rate. When reaching the end point (colour change from red to orange), the tap should be dispensing one drop at a time and slowly. The white tile will aid in observing this colour change.

10 Record the final volume in the burette. Subtract the initial volume from the final volume to calculate the titre volume.

11 Repeat Steps 9 and 10 until concordant titres (highest and lowest values within 0.1 mL) are obtained. **Note:** One drop is the equivalent of 0.05 mL, so it is important your measuring is highly accurate throughout the experiment.

Results

Record your results in Table 1 below.

TABLE 1 Results from the titration

Trial number	Initial volume of burette (mL)	Final volume of burette (mL)	Titre volume (mL)

Discussion

1 Calculate the:

a concentration of the standard Na_2CO_3

b average titre of Na_2CO_3

c amount of Na_2CO_3 that reacted with the HCl

d concentration (mol L^{-1}) of HCl in the aliquot

e concentration (mol L^{-1}) of HCl in the original bottle.

2 What would happen to the concentration that you calculated if there was water in the burette when it was filled with Na_2CO_3?

3 What would happen to the concentration that you calculated if there was water in the pipette when it was filled with the HCl?

4 What would happen to the concentration that you calculated if there was water in the conical flask when it was filled with the HCl?

Determining the concentration of ethanoic acid in white vinegar

CAUTION: ALL CHEMICALS ARE IRRITANTS. SOLID NaOH IS CORROSIVE. WEAR PERSONAL PROTECTIVE EQUIPMENT AT ALL TIMES. IF THE CHEMICALS COME IN CONTACT WITH SKIN, FLUSH THE AFFECTED AREA FOR 15 MINUTES AND CONSULT A HEALTHCARE PROFESSIONAL. IF SPILT, SWEEP INTO A WASTE BIN.

Unit 3, Topic 1: Acid–base titration to calculate the concentration of a solution with reference to a standard solution.

Note: Select Practical 5.1A or Practical 5.1B as the mandatory practical to cover this syllabus point.

Context

White vinegar has an acetic acid (ethanoic acid) content of 4–8% v/v. This means that there is 4–8 mL of the acid per 100 mL of vinegar. Ethanoic acid is a weak acid, so it only partially ionises in water. The reaction of ethanoic acid with the strong base sodium hydroxide (NaOH) has an equivalence point at approximately pH 9. Phenolphthalein is colourless in acidic conditions and turns pink between pH 8.3 and pH 10.0, making it an ideal indicator for this titration.

Ethanoic acid reacts with sodium hydroxide according to the following equation:

$$CH_3COOH(aq) + NaOH(aq) \rightleftharpoons CH_3COONa(aq) + H_2O(l)$$

Note: Over time, sodium hydroxide will absorb carbon dioxide from the atmosphere. Do not leave the solution for longer than a week and assume that it will have the same concentration. It should be used as soon as possible.

Aim

To determine the concentration of ethanoic acid in white vinegar by titration against a standard sodium hydroxide solution, using a phenolphthalein indicator.

Materials

Part A

- 0.8 g pure sodium hydroxide (NaOH) pellets
- 200 mL volumetric flask
- Electronic balance
- Weigh boat
- Spatula
- Wash bottle with deionised water
- Plastic dropping pipette
- Pen for labelling glassware

Part B

- Standard solution of NaOH from Part A
- 25 mL white vinegar
- Phenolphthalein indicator
- 250 mL volumetric flask
- 50 mL burette
- Retort stand and burette clamp (if there is no burette clamp, use a boss head and clamp)
- Funnel
- White tile
- 20.00 mL pipette
- 25.00 mL pipette
- Pipette bulb
- 100 mL beaker for water to wash pipette
- 3 × 100 mL beakers
- 250 mL beaker
- 3 × 100 mL conical flasks
- Wash bottle with deionised water
- Pen for labelling glassware

Method

Part A: Preparation of a standard sodium hydroxide solution

1 Place a weigh boat on the electronic balance and tare it to read zero.
2 Use a spatula to measure 0.8 g of sodium hydroxide pellets into the weigh boat and record its mass. **Note:** This does not need to be exactly 0.8 g, but should be within 0.1 g of 0.8 g.
Never touch NaOH with your bare hands. If there is a spill, follow safety procedures.
3 Wash the volumetric flask with deionised water from the wash bottle. Add the lid, shake the flask and then tip the water down the sink. Repeat this two more times.
4 Add the NaOH pellets to the volumetric flask by scraping them out of the weigh boat with a spatula. There should be no residue to wash from the weigh boat into the flask because the NaOH is in pellet form.
5 Fill the volumetric flask to one-quarter full and swirl the flask until all the NaOH is dissolved. This may take some time because they are pellets and do not have a high surface area.
6 Add deionised water until the bottom of the meniscus is on the mark (this should be on the neck of the flask).
7 Put the lid on the flask and tip the flask upside down and then upright again. Repeat this motion until the solution has an evenly distributed concentration.
8 Label the flask 'NaOH', add its concentration, the date it was prepared and your initials.

Part B: Determining the concentration of an ethanoic acid solution

1 Wash the 250 mL volumetric flask with deionised water from the wash bottle. Add the lid, shake the flask and then tip the water down the sink. Repeat this two more times.
2 Pour some deionised water into a 100 mL beaker and label the beaker 'washing water'. Wash the 25 mL pipette by drawing the washing water up to the mark and then dispensing it down the sink. Repeat this step two more times.
3 Pour 55 mL of white vinegar into a 100 mL beaker and label the beaker 'undiluted vinegar'. Draw 25 mL of the vinegar into the pipette and dispense it into the 250 mL beaker, which should be labelled as 'waste'.
4 Use the 25 mL pipette to dispense 25 mL of the white vinegar into the washed 250 mL volumetric flask. Make the solution up to the mark with deionised water. Add the lid to the flask and tip the flask upside down and then upright again. Repeat this motion until the solution has an evenly distributed concentration.
5 Close the stopcock of the burette and wash it with deionised water from the wash bottle by adding some water and gently tipping the burette onto its side, then slowly spinning it to ensure the water has come in contact with the inside of the burette. Empty some of the water into the sink by tipping the burette upside down and pouring the remaining water out the tip by opening the stopcock. Repeat this one more time.
6 Pour some of the standard NaOH into a 100 mL beaker labelled 'standard NaOH' and repeat Step 5. Only use 10 mL of the solution and do not put the solution down the sink. Dispose of it in the waste beaker. This wash only needs to be performed once.
7 Set up the burette and clamp (see Figure 1).

8 Place the waste beaker under the burette and a funnel on the top. With the stopcock open, pour in the standard solution until no more than 1–2 mL has run through. Then close the stopcock and fill the burette to the top. (**Note:** The burette does not need to be filled to the 0.00 mL line. A final and initial volume will be measured, so it does not matter what value it starts on, as long as it is below 5 mL.) Remove the funnel from the top. Record the initial volume in the burette.

9 Wash the 20 mL pipette as per Step 2 with deionised water. Pour some of the diluted vinegar solution into a 100 mL beaker and label it 'diluted vinegar'. Wash the pipette again with the dilute vinegar solution and dispense it into the waste beaker.

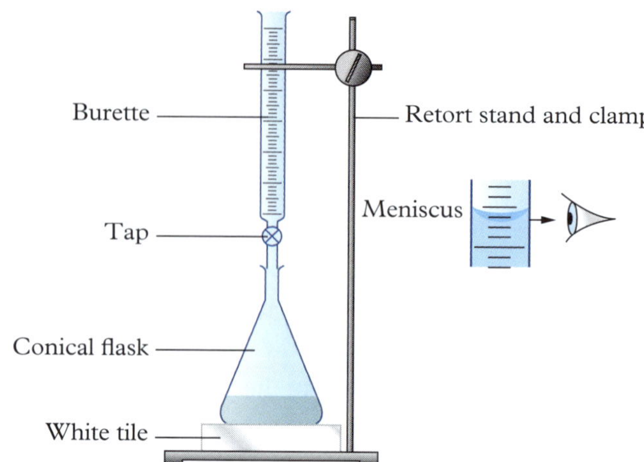

FIGURE 1 The apparatus for the titration

10 Wash the three conical flasks with deionised water and dispense 20 mL of diluted vinegar into each one by using the 20 mL pipette. Add three drops of phenolphthalein into each flask and swirl them. It should result in a colourless solution.

11 Place the first conical flask under the burette and carefully open the stopcock. As the NaOH mixes with the vinegar solution, pink will be visible in the flask. Constantly swirl the flask to remove the pink. After a time, the pink colour will be harder to remove by swirling. Turn the stopcock so that the NaOH solution is dispensed more slowly. When approaching the end point (colour change from colourless to pink), the tap should be dispensing one drop at a time. It will only take one drop to cause the colour change and a pale pink will result. The white tile will aid in observing this colour change.

12 Record the final volume in the burette. Subtract the initial volume from the final volume to calculate the titre volume.

13 Repeat Steps 11 and 12 until concordant titres (highest and lowest values within 0.1 mL) are obtained. **Note:** One drop is the equivalent of 0.05 mL, so it is important your measuring is highly accurate throughout the experiment.

Results

Record your results in Table 1 below.

TABLE 1 Results from the titration

Trial number	Initial volume of burette (mL)	Final volume of burette (mL)	Titre volume (mL)

Discussion

1 Calculate the:

a concentration of the standard NaOH

b average titre of NaOH

c amount of NaOH that reacted with the ethanoic acid

d amount of ethanoic acid in the diluted aliquot

e concentration (mol L^{-1}) of ethanoic acid in the diluted aliquot

f concentration (mol L^{-1}) of ethanoic acid in the original undiluted 25 mL sample

g concentration (g L^{-1}) of ethanoic acid in the original undiluted 25 mL sample

h mass of ethanoic acid in 100 mL of white vinegar

i volume of ethanoic acid in the 100 mL of white vinegar (assume that the density of ethanoic acid is 1.05 g mL^{-1})

j %v/v (volume per 100 mL of vinegar) of ethanoic acid in the white vinegar.

2 What would happen to the concentration that you calculated if there was water in the burette when it was filled with NaOH?

3 What would happen to the concentration that you calculated if there was water in the pipette when it was filled with the diluted vinegar?

4 What would happen to the concentration that you calculated if there was water in the conical flask when it was filled with the diluted vinegar?

5 Compare the result that you calculated with the theoretical concentration (on the bottle or in the introduction). Comment on the precision and accuracy of the results.

6.1 MANDATORY PRACTICAL Performing single displacement reactions

CAUTION: $CuSO_4$ IS TOXIC AND HARMFUL TO THE ENVIRONMENT. WEAR PERSONAL PROTECTIVE EQUIPMENT AT ALL TIMES. IF THE CHEMICAL COMES IN CONTACT WITH SKIN, FLUSH THE AFFECTED AREA FOR 15 MINUTES AND CONSULT A HEALTHCARE PROFESSIONAL. IF SWALLOWED, CONTACT THE POISON CENTRE. CONSULT YOUR LAB TECHNICIAN WHEN DISPOSING OF THIS CHEMICAL. HYDROGEN GAS, WHICH IS HIGHLY FLAMMABLE, IS PRODUCED DURING THIS EXPERIMENT. KEEP AWAY FROM OPEN FLAMES UNTIL READY TO COMBUST.

Unit 3, Topic 4: Perform single displacement reactions in aqueous solutions.

Source: *Chemistry 2019 v1.3 General Senior Syllabus* © Queensland Curriculum & Assessment Authority

Context

Single displacement reactions occur when a stronger reducing agent replaces a weaker reducing agent.

Aim

To perform single displacement reactions and observe any changes.

Materials

- 1 M $CuSO_4$
- Zinc metal strip
- 1 M HCl
- Magnesium metal strip cut into 0.5 cm lengths
- 100 mL beaker
- 2 test tubes
- Test-tube rack
- Matches

Method

Part A

1 Pour 50 mL of 1 M $CuSO_4$ into the 100 mL beaker. Add the zinc metal strip.

2 Observe the changes every 2 minutes for 10 minutes. Record your observations about colour changes, bubbles, appearance of the metal and temperature.

Part B

1 Place five 0.5 cm lengths of magnesium metal strip into a test tube.

2 Add approximately 2–3 cm of 1 M HCl to the test tube and quickly place the second test tube on top (upside down or inverted) to trap any gases produced.

Note: Do not hold the test tube at the bottom; hold it at the top above the solution line.

3 Record your observations about colour changes, bubbles, appearance of the metal and temperature.

4 When the reaction stops producing bubbles, remove the top test tube and keep it inverted (upside down). Light a match and, when ready, hold it at the opening of the test tube.

5 Record any observations of the effects of holding the match under the test tube.

Results

Record your observations in Table 1 on the next page.

TABLE 1 Results from the single displacement reactions

Reaction observations	2 minutes	4 minutes	6 minutes	8 minutes	10 minutes
100 mL beaker					
Colour change					
Bubbles					
Metal appearance					
Temperature					
Test tube					
Colour change					
Bubbles					
Metal appearance					
Temperature					

Discussion

1 Explain what your observations indicate in terms of the reactants and products of both reactions.

2 Write balanced chemical equations for both reactions.

3 Explain why these reactions are displacement reactions.

4 Write half-equations for both reactions.

5 Identify the reduction and oxidation half-equations, as well as the oxidant and reductant in both reactions.

6 Write overall redox equations for both experiments.

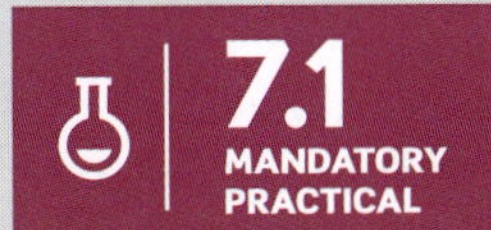

Constructing a galvanic cell

CAUTION: ALL CHEMICALS ARE IRRITANTS. $CuSO_4$ AND $FeCl_2$ ARE CORROSIVE. $Zn(NO_3)_2$ AND KNO_3 ARE FLAMMABLE; KEEP AWAY FROM OPEN FLAMES. WEAR PERSONAL PROTECTIVE EQUIPMENT AT ALL TIMES. IF CHEMICALS COME IN CONTACT WITH SKIN, FLUSH THE AFFECTED AREA FOR 15 MINUTES, AND CONSULT A HEALTHCARE PROFESSIONAL IF ANY CHEMICALS ARE INGESTED. DO NOT DISPOSE OF ANY CHEMICALS DOWN THE SINK. DAMAGED OR EXPOSED WIRES CAN CAUSE SHOCKS. HANDLE WITH CARE.

Unit 3, Topic 2: Construct a galvanic cell using two metal/metal-ion half cells.

Source: *Chemistry 2019 v1.3 General Senior Syllabus* © Queensland Curriculum & Assessment Authority

Context

Galvanic cells are constructed from two half-cells, a salt bridge, connecting wires and a voltmeter. The reducing and oxidising ability of each half-cell determines the amount of energy produced by each cell, and can be measured with the voltmeter. The electrochemical series allows you to predict the outcome of a galvanic cell and the voltage that will result. These half-cells have been measured against the hydrogen half-cell (0.00 V) at 25°C, concentrations of 1 M and 1 atm.

Aim

To determine the order of metals on the electrochemical series by constructing galvanic cells made from various metal/metal-ion half-cells.

Materials

- 50 mL 1 M $CuSO_4$
- 50 mL 1 M $FeCl_2$
- 50 mL 1 M $Zn(NO_3)_2$
- 50 mL 1 M $Al(NO_3)_3$
- 200 mL 1 M KNO_3
- 4 × 100 mL beakers
- Pen for labelling glassware
- One 2 × 10 cm piece of each of the following metals – copper, iron (or a nail), zinc and aluminium
- 6 strips of filter paper (approx. 3 × 15 cm)
- 2 × alligator clips
- Plastic tweezers
- Voltmeter
- Wash bottle with deionised water
- 200 mL waste beaker

Method

1. Construct four half-cells by placing 50 mL of the copper sulfate solution in a 100 mL beaker and adding the copper strip, which acts as the electrode. Repeat this for the iron, zinc and aluminium half-cells. Label each beaker as the respective solution.
2. Dip one piece of the filter paper in the potassium nitrate solution. Using the plastic tweezers, remove it from the solution and place it as a bridge between two of the half-cells.
3. Connect an alligator clip to each of the metal electrodes.
4. Connect the other end of each electrode to the voltmeter. If the voltmeter has a negative reading, swap the wires that are connected to the terminals.

   Note: As soon as the electrodes are connected to the voltmeter, the electrochemical circuit is complete and the voltmeter will immediately measure the voltage of the cell. **This must be recorded immediately because it will reduce over time.**

You must also record whether each electrode is positive or negative in the galvanic cell. This can be determined by looking at the voltmeter. The negative electrode connects to the negative terminal and the positive electrode connects to the positive terminal.

5 Deconstruct the galvanic cell, ensuring that the filter paper is disposed of in the waste beaker and that no solution in the half-cell contaminates another.

6 Reconstruct the galvanic cell until every pair of half-cells has been connected and the results have been recorded.

Results

Record the results for each experiment in Table 1 below.

TABLE 1 Results from the six galvanic cells

Galvanic cell	Metal compound solution	Voltage (V)	Polarity of electrodes
1			
2			
3			
4			
5			
6			

Discussion

1 Which electrode is always negative, and which is always positive? Use this information to list the half-cells in order with the strongest oxidant first.

2 Does your half-cell order agree with the half-equations on the electrochemical series?

3 Use the electrochemical series to draw the six galvanic cells. You must also add the E° of each cell.

4 Do the theoretical and experimental E° values match? Explain why this is.

5 What is the salt bridge in the experiment? Explain why this ionic solution was selected as the salt bridge.

6 On the electrochemical series, copper is the highest half-equation because copper ions are the strongest oxidant. What materials can be used to construct a copper half-cell if it is connected to a tin half-cell? Explain why you chose these materials.

8.1A SUGGESTED PRACTICAL Electrolysis of water

CAUTION: ALL CHEMICALS ARE IRRITANTS. KOH IS HIGHLY CORROSIVE IN CONTACT WITH SKIN. GLOVES NEED TO BE WORN AT ALL TIMES. IF THE CHEMICALS COME IN CONTACT WITH SKIN, FLUSH THE AFFECTED AREA FOR 15 MINUTES, AND CONSULT A HEALTHCARE PROFESSIONAL IF ANY CHEMICALS ARE INGESTED. CONSULT YOUR LAB TECHNICIAN WHEN DISPOSING OF CHEMICALS. DAMAGED OR EXPOSED WIRES CAN CAUSE SHOCKS. HANDLE WITH CARE.

Unit 3, Topic 2: Carry out electrolysis of water or copper sulfate. Simulations could be used.

Source: *Chemistry 2019 v1.3 General Senior Syllabus* © Queensland Curriculum & Assessment Authority

Aim

To construct a simple model of an electrolytic cell and an alkaline fuel cell.

Materials

- 250 mL 1 M KOH solution
- Power supply
- 3 × wires with crocodile clips
- 100 mL measuring cylinder
- Retort stand and retort ring
- 2 × semi-micro test tubes
- Voltmeter
- Plastic cup with two carbon rods embedded in the bottom and sealed with a sealant so that there are no leaks. **Note:** Ensure that the cup fits in the retort ring and does not slip through it.

Method

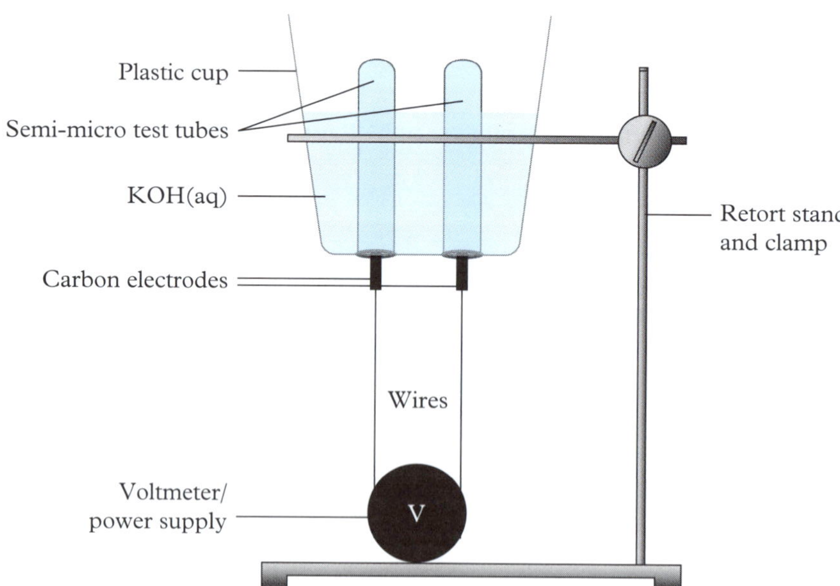

FIGURE 1 Experimental set-up of an electrolytic cell and alkaline fuel cell

1 Set up the retort stand with the retort ring as shown in Figure 1. Place the plastic cup fuel cell in the retort ring.
2 Pour the 1 M KOH solution into the cup so that the solution covers the electrodes.
3 Completely fill each semi-micro test tube with 1 M KOH solution, and, wearing gloves, hold a finger over the top of the test tube. Turn it upside down, and place it in the KOH solution and over the carbon rod. Repeat for the other electrode ensuring that there are no bubbles in the test tubes.
4 Use the alligator clips to connect the carbon rods to the power supply. Turn the power supply to 6 V and switch the power on for 5 minutes.

   Note: Do not allow the test tube to be completely filled with gas; there must be some KOH electrolyte left touching the carbon rods.
5 Turn the power off when the test tube containing the largest volume of gas is three-quarters full.
6 Disconnect the electrodes from the power supply and reconnect them to the voltmeter. Record the immediate voltage in Table 1.

Results

1 Draw a fully labelled diagram of the fuel cell in discharge, including half- and overall equations.

2 Draw a fully labelled diagram of the electrolytic cell in recharge, including half- and overall equations.

3 Record your results in Table 1 below.

TABLE 1 Results from the electrolytic and alkaline fuel cells

Experiment	Observations	Voltage (V)
Power supply connected		
Spontaneous/discharge		

Discussion

1 In electrolysis, compare the volume of gases in the test tubes. What justification can you give for their volumes?

2 Why shouldn't you allow the gas to completely fill the electrodes?

3 What are the environmental issues associated with generating the gases in electrolysis?

4 How does the theoretical E° value compare with the experimental E° value? How could any difference in the values be explained?

5 What is the difference between the fuel cell used in this experiment and a fuel cell used for larger purposes, such as for a space shuttle?

8.1B SUGGESTED PRACTICAL

Electroplating of copper

CAUTION: ALL CHEMICALS ARE IRRITANTS. $CuSO_4$ IS TOXIC AND AN IRRITANT. WEAR PERSONAL PROTECTIVE EQUIPMENT AT ALL TIMES. IF THE CHEMICALS COME IN CONTACT WITH SKIN, FLUSH THE AFFECTED AREA FOR 15 MINUTES, AND CONSULT A HEALTHCARE PROFESSIONAL IF ANY CHEMICALS ARE INGESTED. CONSULT YOUR LAB TECHNICIAN WHEN DISPOSING OF CHEMICALS. DAMAGED OR EXPOSED WIRES CAN CAUSE SHOCKS. HANDLE WITH CARE.

Unit 3, Topic 2: Use an electrolytic cell to carry out metal plating.

Source: *Chemistry 2019 v1.3 General Senior Syllabus* © Queensland Curriculum & Assessment Authority

Aim

The purpose of this experiment is to observe and measure the effects of electroplating copper onto a copper cathode.

Materials

- 60 mL 1 M $CuSO_4$ solution
- 2 × copper strips (approx. 7 cm × 3 cm)
- 50 mL acetone
- Wash bottle with deionised water
- DC power supply
- 2 × 100 mL beakers
- 200 mL waste beaker
- 2 × wires with crocodile clips
- Sheet of emery paper
- Electronic balance
- Stopwatch

Method

1 Use the emery paper to clean the electrodes. Wash them with the wash bottle. Fill a 100 mL beaker with acetone and dip the electrodes into it. Allow the electrodes to air dry.

2 Weigh both electrodes by using the balance and record their mass in Table 1. Make a note of the one you will use as the anode and cathode.

3 Pour 60 mL of 1 M $CuSO_4$ into a 100 mL beaker and add the electrodes.

4 Connect the cathode to the negative terminal of the power supply and the anode to the positive terminal, using the wires with crocodile clips (see Figure 1).

   Note: It may be easier to curve the electrode around the mouth of the beaker so that it is hooked onto its side. In this way, the electrodes will not touch one another and remain a constant distance apart.

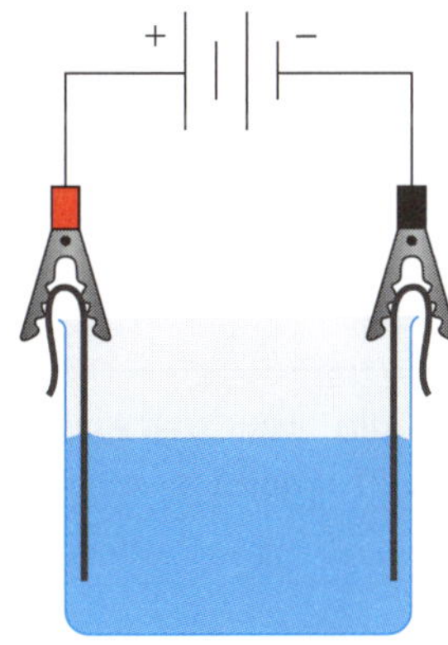

FIGURE 1 Experimental set-up of an electroplating cell

5 Turn the settings of the power supply to 8 V. Ensure that the stopwatch is ready to start timing. Turn the power supply on and start timing for 10 minutes.

6 Turn the power supply off and disconnect the electrodes.

7 Remove the cathode and use the wash bottle to wash the copper sulfate solution remaining on the electrode into the waste beaker. Add acetone to the 100 mL beaker and dip the cathode into the beaker, allowing it to air dry.

8 Once completely dry, use the balance to weigh the electrode and record its mass in Table 1.

9 Repeat Steps 7 and 8 with the anode.

Results

Record your results in Table 1 below.

TABLE 1 Results of the electroplating cell

Electrode	Mass of the electrode (g)		
	Before electrolysis	After electrolysis	Change in mass
Cathode			
Anode			

Discussion

1 Compare the mass difference in the anode and cathode.

2 Write a fully labelled cell diagram with half- and overall equations to demonstrate the processes occurring within the electrolytic cell.

3 Could other materials be used as the anode or cathode? Explain your answer using the electrochemical series.

4 Could another solution have been used as the electrolyte? Explain your answer.

9.3 SUGGESTED PRACTICAL Interpreting 2D and 3D functional groups

Unit 4, Topic 1: Identify different typical functional groups in molecules.

Source: *Chemistry 2019 v1.3 General Senior Syllabus* © Queensland Curriculum & Assessment Authority

Aim

To construct 3D models of complex organic molecules.

Materials

- 3D modelling kit for organic chemistry

Method

1 The 3D modelling kit has balls with different colours and number of holes. Identify the following. Carbon atoms have four holes and are usually black. Oxygen atoms have two holes and are usually red. Hydrogen atoms have one hole and are usually white. Nitrogen atoms have three holes and are usually blue. Halogen atoms have one hole and are usually green.

2 Construct the molecules given in Table 1 below, using their two-dimensional diagrams. Identify each of the functional groups present, in order of priority, and write them in Table 1.

TABLE 1 Complex organic molecules

Molecular name	Applications	Two-dimensional diagram	Functional groups present
Limonene	Citrus peel	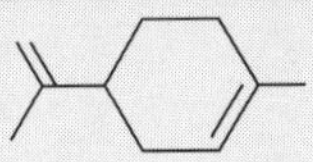	
Glucose	Sugar	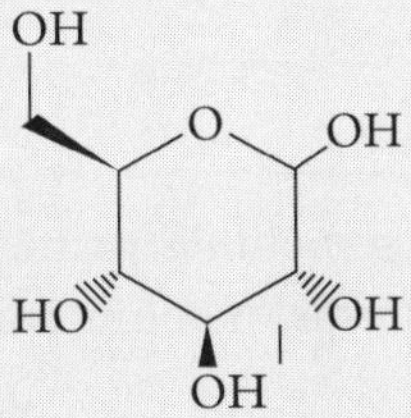 OH, O, OH, HO, OH, OH	
Amphetamine	ADHD medication	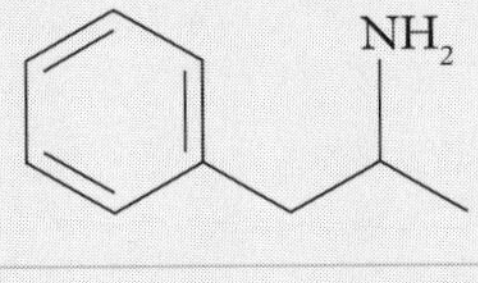 NH_2	
Paracetamol	Pain medication	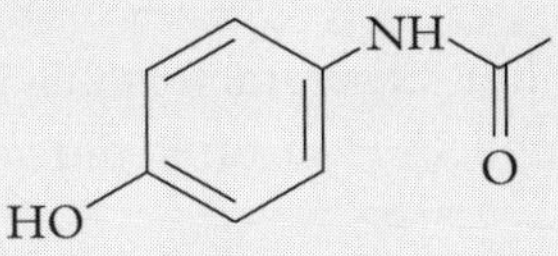 NH, O, HO	
Vanillin	Vanilla extract	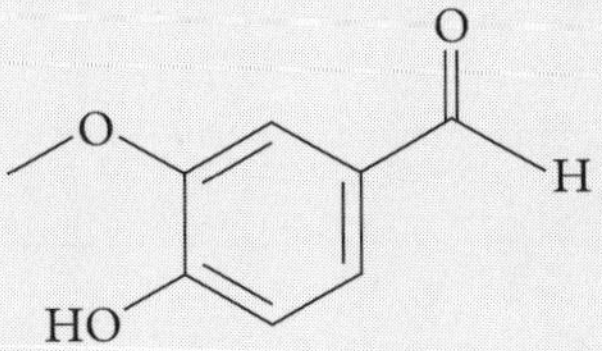 O, O, H, HO	

Molecular name	Applications	Two-dimensional diagram	Functional groups present
Vitamin C	Vitamin	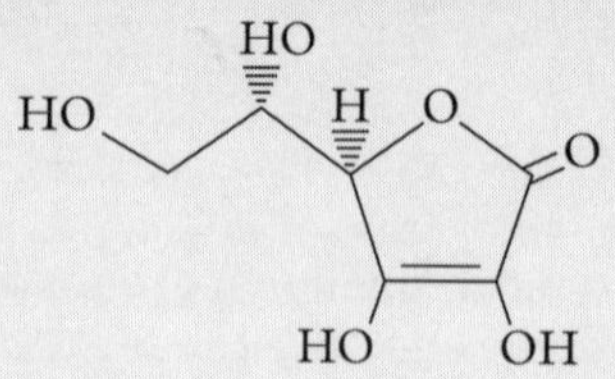	
Adrenalin	Stress hormone	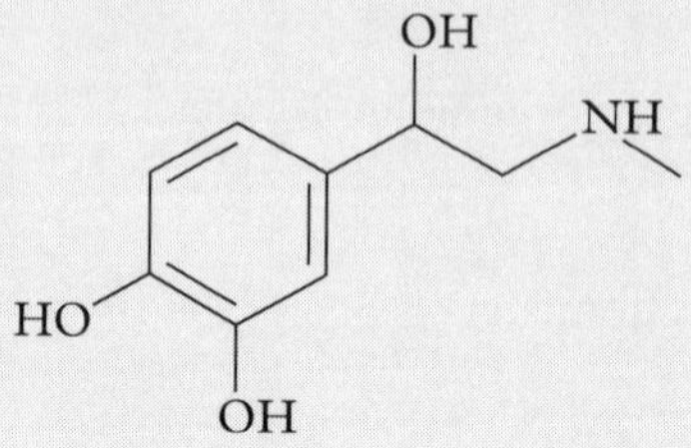	
Citalopram	Antidepressant	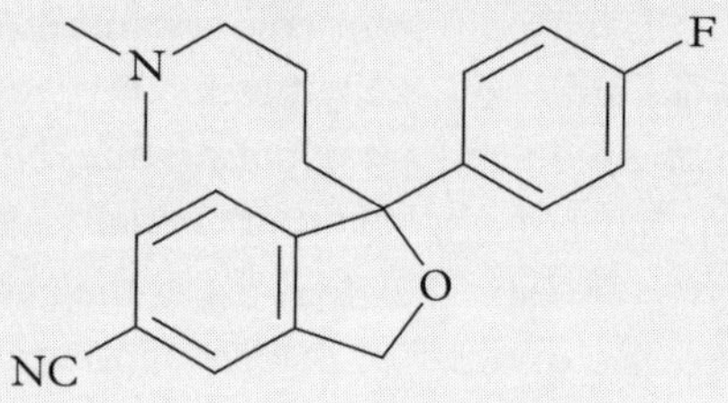	

Discussion

1 Identify the most common functional groups present in the complex organic molecules provided (Table 1).

2 The hydroxy functional group was sometimes written backwards in the two-dimensional diagrams. Evaluate the significance of this in terms of communicating accurate representations of bonding.

3 Evaluate the effectiveness of the line structural formula in terms of providing adequate information to make the three-dimensional models. How often did you miscount the number of carbon and hydrogen atoms?

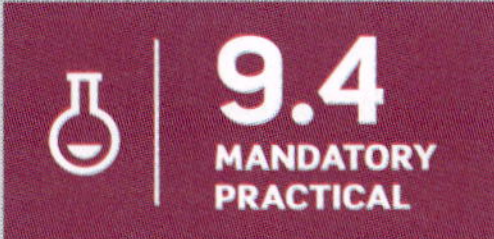

Modelling isomers of organic molecules

Unit 4, Topic 1: Construct 3D models of organic molecules.

Source: *Chemistry 2019 v1.3 General Senior Syllabus* © Queensland Curriculum & Assessment Authority

Context

The covalent bonding between carbon and other elements involves sharing electrons. The spatial arrangement reflects the number of bonding and non-bonding electrons that each element has. Although a two-dimensional representation of this is helpful, three-dimensional modelling provides much more information. In particular, isomers are best seen in three dimensions.

Aim

To construct 3D models of esters, amides, amines and isomers.

Materials

- 3D modelling kit for organic chemistry

Method

1 The 3D modelling kit has balls with different colours and number of holes. Identify the following:
   - Carbon atoms have four holes and are usually black.
   - Oxygen atoms have two holes and are usually red.
   - Hydrogen atoms have one hole and are usually white.
   - Nitrogen atoms have three holes and are usually blue.
   - Halogen atoms have one hole and are usually green.

2 Construct methyl propanoate from 4 black carbon, 2 red oxygen, 8 white hydrogen, 12 short bonds and 2 long bonds (for the double bond). Using the same atoms and bonds, construct two other structural isomers of methyl propanoate. Draw the condensed and line structural formulas, and name each structural isomer below.

3 Construct *N*-ethylethanamide from 4 black carbon, 1 red oxygen, 9 white hydrogen, 1 blue nitrogen, 13 short bonds and 2 long bonds. Using the same atoms and bonds, construct two other structural isomers of *N*-ethylethanamide. Draw the condensed and line structural formulas, and name each structural isomer below.

4 Construct as many viable organic molecules as possible from 3 black carbon, 9 white hydrogen, 1 blue nitrogen and 12 short bonds. Draw the condensed and line structural formulas, and name each structural isomer below.

5 Construct two enantiomers of 1-bromoethan-1-ol from 4 black carbon, 10 white hydrogen, 2 red oxygen, 2 green bromine and 16 short bonds. Rotate the two molecules and sit them closely together to test whether they can be superimposed. Draw the enantiomers below, using dashed and solid wedged bonds.

Discussion

1 Explain why the two holes in the oxygen atom were not on opposite sides of the red ball.

2 Evaluate the significance of the types of isomerism, in terms of changing the properties of substances.

3 Explain why there are only ever two enantiomers of a compound with a single chiral atom.

4 The atoms, and groups of atoms, in the molecular models were able to rotate around and constantly shift the spatial arrangement of the molecule itself. Discuss how the lack of flexibility in a double bond leads to the possibility of geometrical isomerism.

Bromination of unsaturated hydrocarbons

CAUTION: TEACHER-ONLY DEMONSTRATION! ALL CHEMICALS ARE IRRITANTS. THE ORGANIC COMPOUNDS ARE TOXIC AND IRRITANTS. WEAR PERSONAL PROTECTIVE EQUIPMENT AT ALL TIMES AND COMPLETE THE EXPERIMENT IN A FUME CUPBOARD. NO CHEMICALS ARE TO BE HANDLED BY STUDENTS. IF THE CHEMICALS COME IN CONTACT WITH SKIN, FLUSH THE AFFECTED AREA FOR 15 MINUTES, AND CONSULT A HEALTHCARE PROFESSIONAL IF ANY CHEMICALS ARE INGESTED. CONSULT YOUR LAB TECHNICIAN WHEN DISPOSING OF CHEMICALS.

Unit 4, Topic 1: Chemical tests to distinguish between alkanes and alkenes.

Source: *Chemistry 2019 v1.3 General Senior Syllabus* © Queensland Curriculum & Assessment Authority

Aim

To compare the reactivity of cyclohexane and cyclohexene with bromine.

Materials

- 1 mL cyclohexene
- 1 mL cyclohexane
- 2% solution of bromine water
- 2 test tubes with a test-tube rack
- 3 disposable pipettes

Method

1. Transfer 1 mL of cyclohexane into the first test tube by using a disposable pipette. Take note of its appearance in Table 1.
2. Transfer 1 mL of cyclohexene into the second test tube by using another disposable pipette. Take note of its appearance in Table 1.
3. Add 1 mL of bromine water to the first test tube by using the third disposable pipette (add it dropwise and down the side of the test tube). Take note of its appearance in Table 1.
4. Add 1 mL of bromine water to the second test tube by using the third disposable pipette (add it dropwise and down the side of the test tube). Take note of its appearance in Table 1.
5. Gently shake both test tubes, allowing the two layers in the test tubes to mix well. Take note of any changes that occur in Table 1.
6. Empty the test tubes into an organic waste container, rinsing with an organic solvent such as acetone.

Results

Record the results in Table 1.

TABLE 1 Changes in appearance of the hydrocarbons

Hydrocarbon	Stage	Observation
Cyclohexane	Before the bromine was added	
	After the bromine was added	
	After the test tube was gently shaken	

Cyclohexene	Before the bromine was added	
	After the bromine was added	
	After the test tube was gently shaken	

Discussion

1 Identify which test tube had a positive result and which test tube had a negative result. Justify your response with a balanced chemical equation.

____

____

____

2 Explain the presence of two layers when the bromine was added to the hydrocarbons.

____

____

____

3 Predict the structure of the brominated hydrocarbon. Draw an extended structural formula of the product and name it by using IUPAC rules.

4 Evaluate the limitations of this reaction as a chemical test. Does it work on all unsaturated hydrocarbons? Does it always give a negative result for saturated hydrocarbons?

____

____

____

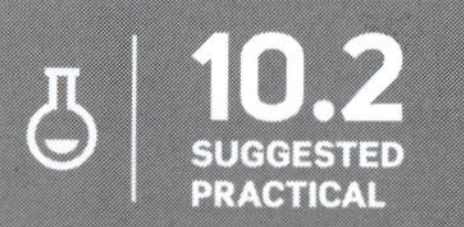

10.2 SUGGESTED PRACTICAL Oxidation of alcohols

CAUTION: TEACHER-ONLY DEMONSTRATION! ALL CHEMICALS ARE IRRITANTS. WEAR PERSONAL PROTECTIVE EQUIPMENT AT ALL TIMES AND COMPLETE THE EXPERIMENT IN A FUME CUPBOARD. NO CHEMICALS ARE TO BE HANDLED BY STUDENTS. IF THE CHEMICALS COME IN CONTACT WITH SKIN, FLUSH THE AFFECTED AREA FOR 15 MINUTES, AND CONSULT A HEALTHCARE PROFESSIONAL IF ANY CHEMICALS ARE INGESTED. CONSULT YOUR LAB TECHNICIAN WHEN DISPOSING OF CHEMICALS.

Unit 4, Topic 1: Chemical tests to distinguish primary, secondary and tertiary alcohols.

Source: *Chemistry 2019 v1.3 General Senior Syllabus* © Queensland Curriculum & Assessment Authority

Aim

To compare the reactivity of primary, secondary and tertiary alcohols.

Materials

- 10 mL ethanol
- 10 mL butan-2-ol
- 10 mL 2-methylpropan-2-ol
- 15 mL 0.015 M $K_2Cr_2O_7$ (in 3 M H_2SO_4)
- 15 mL 0.1 M $KMnO_4$ (in 1 M H_2SO_4)
- 6 test tubes with a test-tube rack
- 10 mL measuring cylinder
- 5 disposable pipettes

Method

1. Add 5 mL of ethanol to the first test tube, 5 mL of butan-2-ol to the second test tube, and 5 mL of 2-methylpropan-2-ol to the third test tube. Take note of their appearance in Table 1.
2. Add 5 mL of acidified potassium dichromate solution to each of the three test tubes. Gently shake the test tubes, observing their appearance over time. Take note of any changes that occur in Table 1.
3. Add 5 mL of ethanol to the fourth test tube, 5 mL of butan-2-ol to the fifth test tube, and 5 mL of 2-methylpropan-2-ol to the sixth test tube. Take note of their appearance in Table 1.
4. Add 5 mL of acidified potassium permanganate solution to each of the three test tubes. Gently shake the test tubes, observing their appearance over time. Take note of any changes that occur in Table 1.
5. Empty the test tubes into an organic waste container, rinsing the test tubes with an organic solvent such as acetone.

Results

Record the results in Table 1.

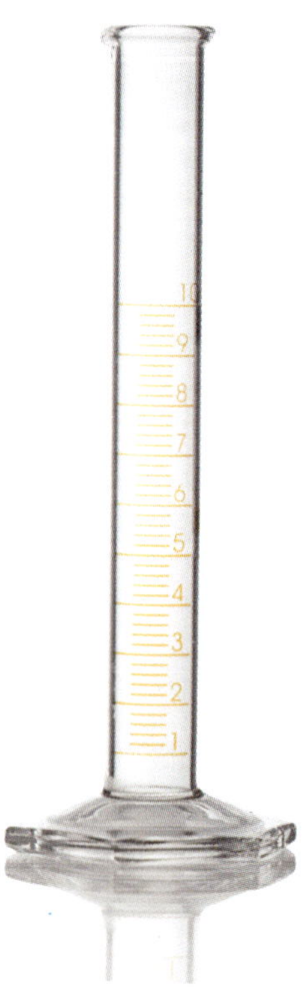

FIGURE 1 Measuring cyclinder

TABLE 1 Changes in appearance of the alcohols

Alcohol	Observation of potassium dichromate reaction		Observation of potassium permanganate reaction	
Ethanol	Before		Before	
	After		After	
Butan-2-ol	Before		Before	
	After		After	
2-Methylpropan-2-ol	Before		Before	
	After		After	

Discussion

1 Identify which test tubes had a positive result and which test tubes had a negative result.

2 Predict the structure of the oxidised products. Draw an extended structural formula of the products and name them by using IUPAC rules.

3 Balance the redox reactions of the primary and secondary alcohols using the half-equation method in acidic conditions.

4 Evaluate the limitations of these reactions as a chemical test. Do they work on all primary and secondary alcohols? Does it always give a negative result for tertiary alcohols?

11.3 SUGGESTED PRACTICAL

Catalysing decomposition reactions

CAUTION: H_2O_2 IS A MILD IRRITANT. WEAR PERSONAL PROTECTIVE EQUIPMENT AT ALL TIMES AND COMPLETE THE EXPERIMENT IN A FUME CUPBOARD. IF THE CHEMICALS COME IN CONTACT WITH SKIN, FLUSH THE AFFECTED AREA FOR 15 MINUTES, AND CONSULT A HEALTHCARE PROFESSIONAL IF ANY CHEMICALS ARE INGESTED. CONSULT YOUR LAB TECHNICIAN WHEN DISPOSING OF CHEMICALS.

Unit 4, Topic 1: Use enzymes as catalysts.

Source: *Chemistry 2019 v1.3 General Senior Syllabus* © Queensland Curriculum & Assessment Authority

Aim

To determine the rate of decomposition reaction of hydrogen peroxide, when catalysed by the enzyme catalase.

Materials

- Vernier O_2 gas sensor
- Vernier LabQuest® interface (or LabQuest® Mini attached to a computer)
- 250 mL Vernier BioChamber with one opening (or 250 mL conical flask sealed with parafilm)
- 10 mL measuring cylinder
- Wash bottle with deionised water
- 5% solution of hydrogen peroxide (H_2O_2)
- Disposable pipette
- Suspension of catalase

Method

1. Connect the gas sensor to the LabQuest® interface and start the data collection software. Select a new file. The software will detect the type of sensor attached and prepare for data collection.
2. Place 5 mL of deionised water and 5 mL of hydrogen peroxide in the BioChamber.
3. Add 20 drops of the enzyme suspension to the BioChamber by using the disposable pipette, immediately sealing with the gas sensor.
4. Select the collect button to begin data collection of the percentage of gaseous oxygen in the BioChamber.
5. When the reaction has finished, remove the gas sensor from the BioChamber and disconnect the LabQuest® interface. Rinse the BioChamber with water and use a paper towel to dry it.

Results

Select the linear region of the collected data and press the linear fit button, followed by 'OK'. Graph the experimental data, using time (in minutes) as the x-axis and concentration of oxygen gas (as %) as the y-axis. This can either be drawn by hand on your own paper or printed off the interface with the linear regression line and gradient. The gradient of the graph is the rate of oxygen production per minute.

Discussion

1 Describe the data collected over time. Is the gradient consistent across the whole experiment, or does it change value? Link your knowledge of collision theory to explain the experimental data.

2 Using your knowledge of catalysts, sketch an energy profile diagram of the decomposition reaction with and without catalase.

3 Evaluate the success of the experiment. Is the data sufficient enough to make a valid conclusion? Are there any limitations in the experiment? What would you do to make the experiment more valid?

Identifying amino acids by paper chromatography

CAUTION: THE CHROMATOGRAPHY SOLVENT AND NINHYDRIN ARE FLAMMABLE AND TOXIC. HCl AND AMINO ACIDS ARE IRRITANTS. WEAR PERSONAL PROTECTIVE EQUIPMENT AT ALL TIMES. IF THE CHEMICALS COME IN CONTACT WITH SKIN, FLUSH THE AFFECTED AREA FOR 15 MINUTES, AND CONSULT A HEALTHCARE PROFESSIONAL IF ANY CHEMICALS ARE INGESTED. CONSULT YOUR LAB TECHNICIAN WHEN DISPOSING OF CHEMICALS.

Unit 4, Topic 1: Separate and identify components of amino acid mixtures using chromatography and or electrophoresis. Simulations could be used. Data loggers could be used.

Source: *Chemistry 2019 v1.3 General Senior Syllabus* © Queensland Curriculum & Assessment Authority

Aim

To separate amino acids using paper chromatography and to identify an unknown amino acid by comparison of R_f values.

Materials

- Beaker and watch glass for lid
- Chromatography paper
- Spotting tubes (blunt-ended needles or plastic micropipette tips are good for this purpose)
- Chromatography solvent: 60% butanol, 15% acetic acid and 25% water, by volume (this should be made fresh on the day of the experiment)
- Hair dryer (alternately, chromatography papers can be dried and developed in a laboratory oven)
- Gloves
- Spray bottle of 1% ninhydrin (indanetrione) in acetone
- Labelled amino acid samples of alanine, serine and methionine as their zwitterions (not hydrochloride salts) in ethanol, as filtered, saturated solutions
- Unknown amino acid mixtures for separation and identification

Method

1 Using gloves, collect a chromatography paper, cut to match the beaker dimensions.

2 Draw with a pencil a baseline across the paper rectangle. Mark four small dots, at equal distances across the line and label each dot 'A', 'S', 'M' and 'U'. Draw another parallel line about 4 cm above the baseline.

3 Carefully dip the spotter into the amino acid solution containing alanine. Touch the tip to the small dot on the chromatography paper labelled 'A'. Repeat this process for the other amino acids and the unknown mixture, using a clean spotting tube each time.

4 In the fume cupboard, pour 10 mL of chromatography solvent into the beaker. Using a pair of tweezers, carefully lower your chromatography paper into the beaker, spot end down, to stand up in the beaker, making sure that the spots are not submerged.

5 Put the watch glass over the top of the beaker. Wait about 20 minutes, and carefully remove the paper with your tweezers and gently dab dry the bottom of the paper on a paper towel. Use the hair dryer to dry the chromatography paper.

6 Amino acids are colourless, so they need to be sprayed with ninhydrin to form coloured compounds. Do this in the fume cupboard and then dry the sheet with a hair dryer until the spots appear.

Identify the contents of the unknown solution by comparing the position of the spots with the spots of the standard samples. Measure the distance from the baseline to the centre of each spot. If the spots are faint, they can be enhanced by photocopying the paper with the contrast adjusted.

Results

Record your results in Table 1 below.

TABLE 1 Identification of amino acids by using paper chromatography

Amino acid	R_f value	Colour of spot observed
Alanine (A)		
Serine (S)		
Methionine (M)		
Unknown mixture (first spot)		
Unknown mixture (second spot)		

Discussion

1 What is the unknown amino acid?

2 How confident could you be in the identification of the amino acids in your unknown mixture? What would be some possible ways to improve the separation of the amino acids?

3 Chromatography involves separation by competition between a stationary phase (chromatography paper here) and a mobile phase (the chromatography solvent). What do the relative R_f values tell you about the interactions of each amino acid with the stationary phase and the mobile phase?

Using mass spectrometry and infrared spectroscopy to identify organic compounds

Unit 4, Topic 1: Identify organic compounds using mass spectrometry and infrared. Simulations could be used.

Source: *Chemistry 2019 v1.3 General Senior Syllabus* © Queensland Curriculum & Assessment Authority

Aim

To identify organic compounds by matching mass spectra and infrared spectra data.

Materials

- QCAA Chemistry formula and data book

Method and Results

1 Study the mass spectra (EI, electron ionisation) and infrared spectra in Figures 1 to 16.

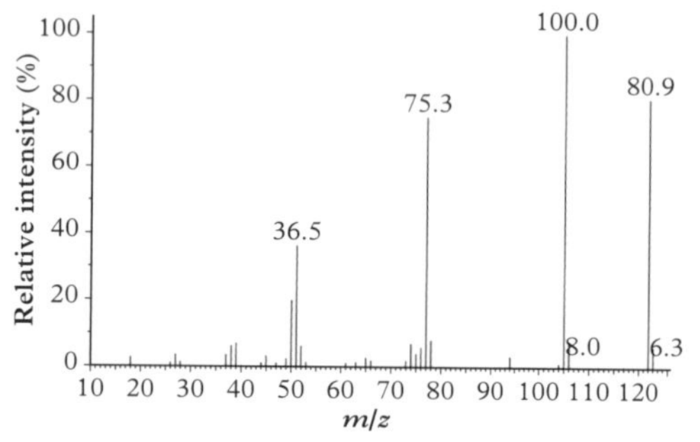

FIGURE 1 Mass spectrum 1

Relative intensity (%)
100
80
60
40
20
0
100.0
16.9
8.6
5.9 5.7
10 20 30 40 50 60 70 80 90 100 110 120 130 140 150 160 170
m/z

FIGURE 2 Mass spectrum 2

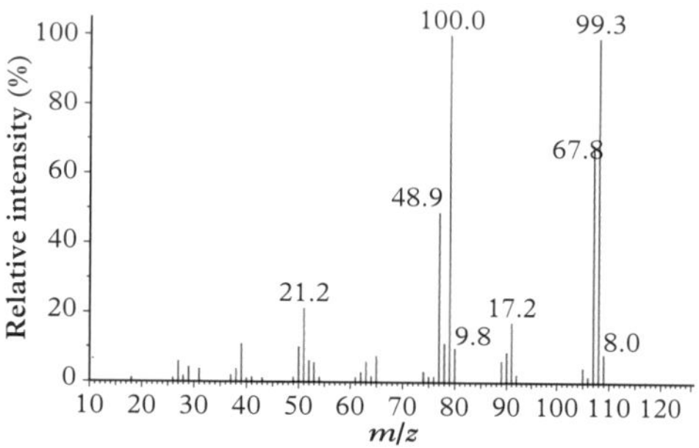

FIGURE 3 Mass spectrum 3

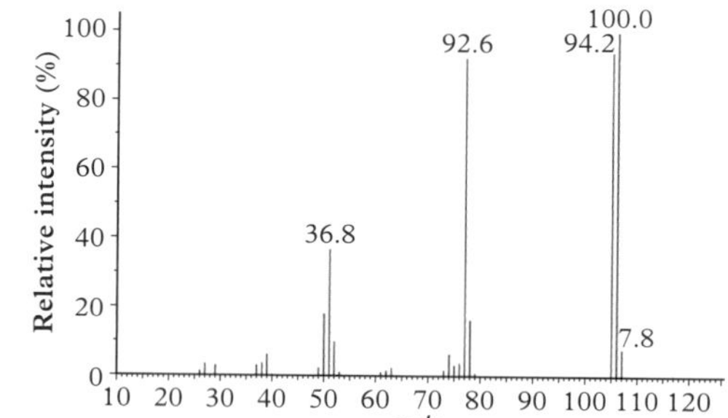

FIGURE 4 Mass spectrum 4

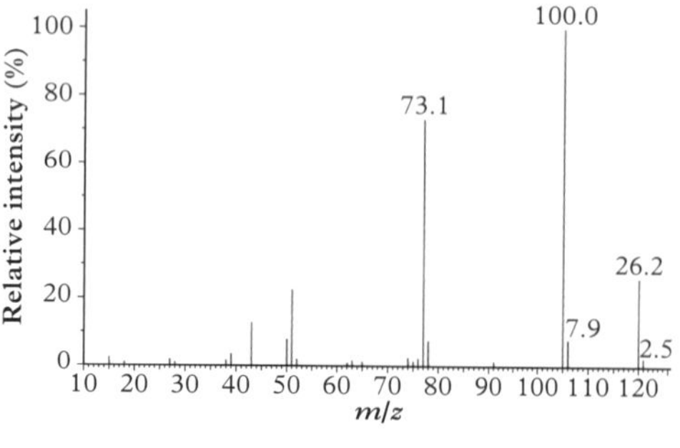

FIGURE 5 Mass spectrum 5

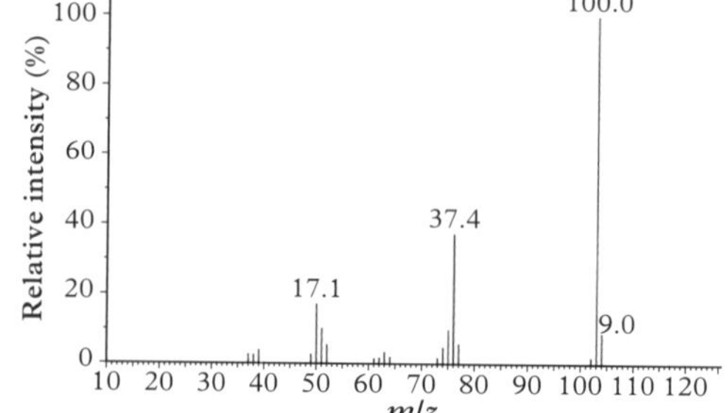

FIGURE 6 Mass spectrum 6

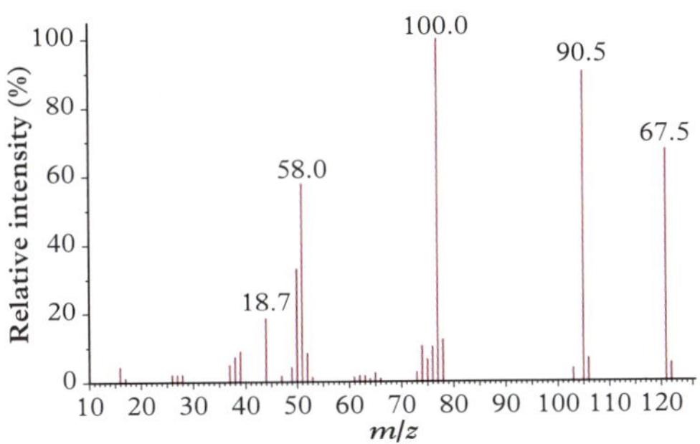

FIGURE 7 Mass spectrum 7

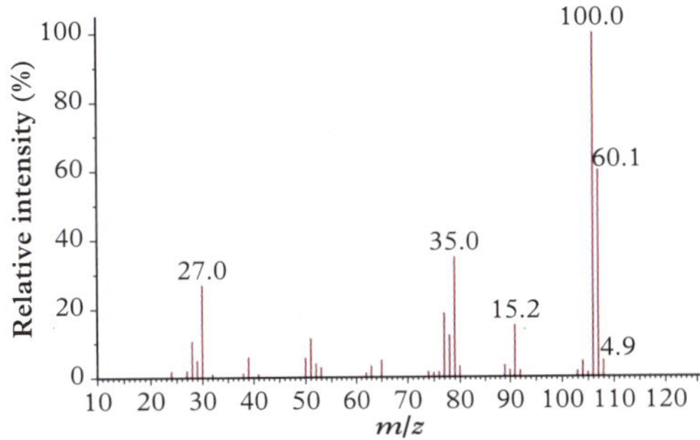

FIGURE 8 Mass spectrum 8

Infrared spectra (bands: s = strong, m = medium, w = weak, br = broad)

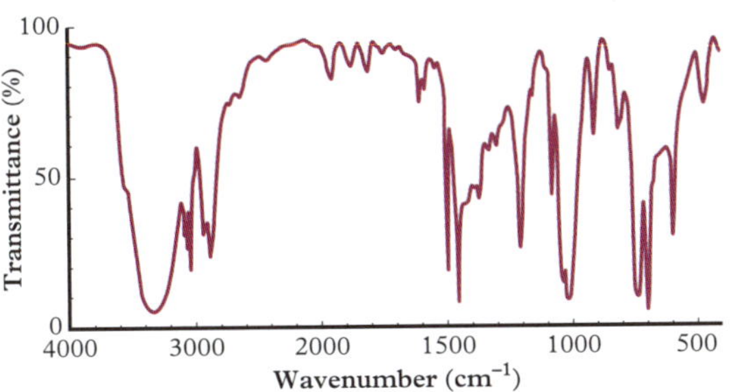

FIGURE 9 Infrared spectrum 1. Important bands: 3326 (s, br), 3088 (m), 3066 (m), 3031 (m), 2932 (m), 2875 (m), 1497 (s), 1454 (s), 1018 (s), 736 (s), 698 (s) cm^{-1}.

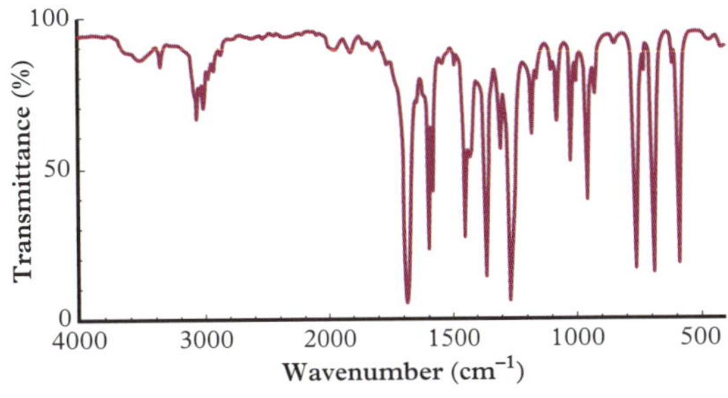

FIGURE 10 Infrared spectrum 2. Important bands: 3087 (w), 3063 (w), 3040 (w), 1686 (s), 1599 (s), 1450 (s), 1360 (s), 1267 (s), 761 (s), 691 (s) cm^{-1}.

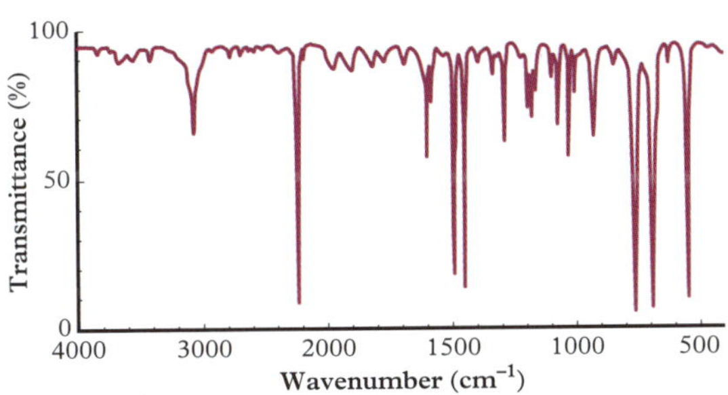

FIGURE 11 Infrared spectrum 3. Important bands: 3066 (m), 2230 (s), 1599 (m), 1492 (s), 1448 (s), 758 (s), 688 (s), 549 (s) cm^{-1}.

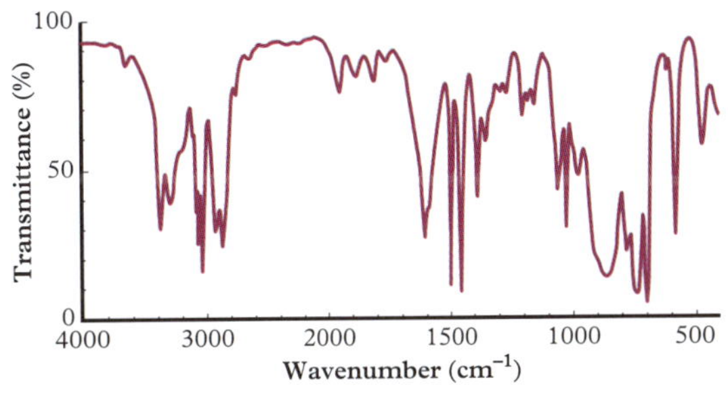

FIGURE 12 Infrared spectrum 4. Important bands: 3373 (m), 3290 (m), 3085 (m), 3062 (m), 3027 (s), 2920 (m), 2859 (m), 1805 (m), 1686 (m), 1496 (s), 1453 (s), 866 (s), 782 (s), 739 (s), 698 (s) cm^{-1}.

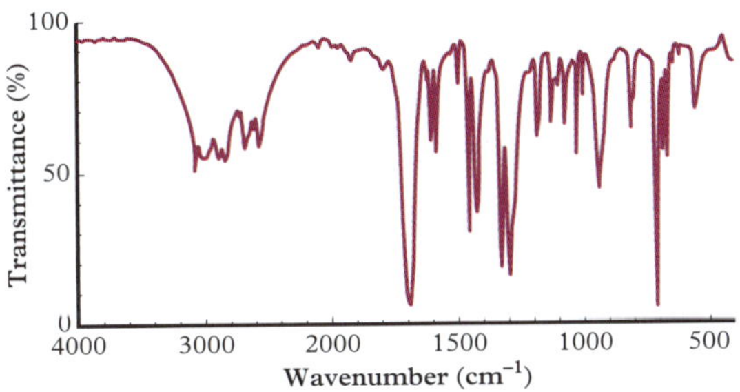

FIGURE 13 Infrared spectrum 5. Important bands: 3012 (m), 2998 (m), 2986 (m), 1688 (s), 1454 (m), 1327 (s), 1294 (s), 708 (s) cm^{-1}.

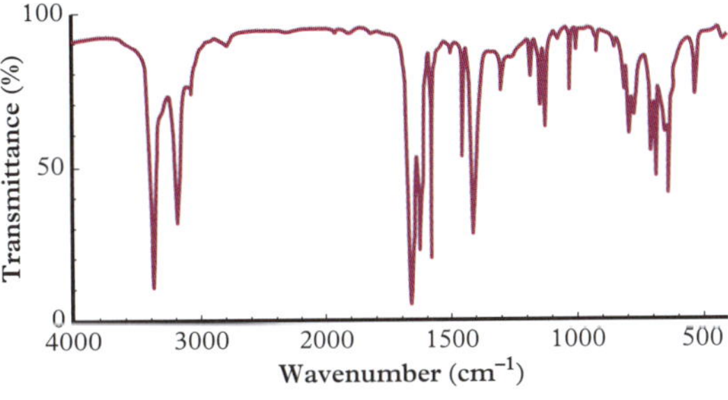

FIGURE 14 Infrared spectrum 6. Important bands: 3369 (s), 3177 (m), 1661 (s), 1626 (s), 1579 (s), 1405 (m), 706 (m), 686 (m), 637 (m) cm^{-1}.

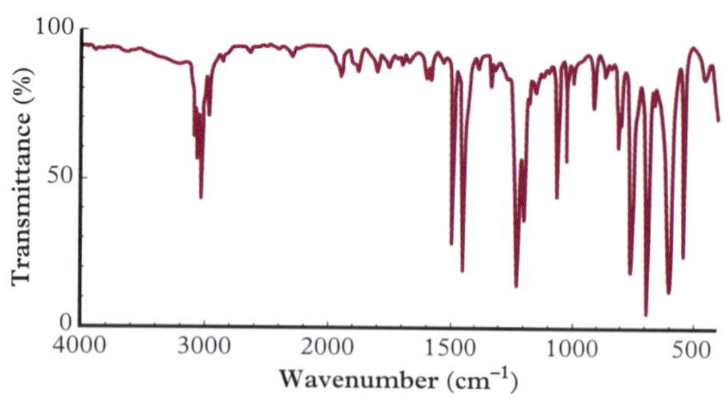

FIGURE 15 Infrared spectrum 7. Important bands: 3031 (m), 1496 (s), 1454 (s), 1227 (s), 1201 (s), 758 (s), 695 (s), 606 (s) cm^{-1}.

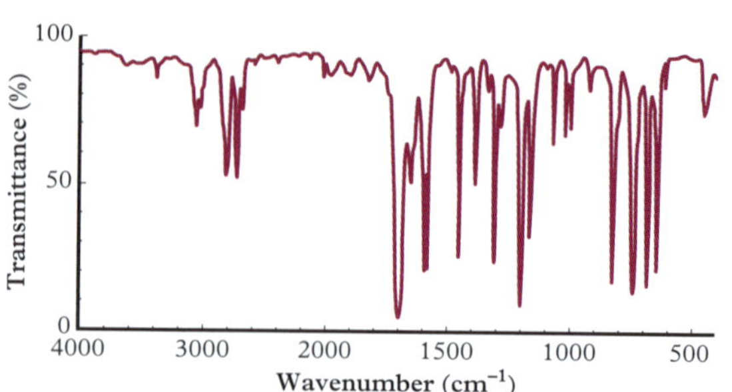

FIGURE 16 Infrared spectrum 8. Important bands: 3065 (w), 2820 (m), 2738 (m), 1703 (s), 1311 (s), 1204 (s), 828 (s), 746 (s), 688 (s), 650 (s) cm^{-1}.

2 For each mass spectrum, answer the following questions and record your answers in Table 1 below.

   a What is the *m*/*z* value for each molecular ion for each of the mass spectra?

   b Use the 'rule of 13' to work out the base value for this *m*/*z* value (i.e. how many C and H atoms would this compound have, if it only contained C and H).

   c Does the compound contain Cl or Br? (Yes/No)

   d Does the compound contain an odd number of N atoms? (Yes/No)

   e What is the suspected organic compound?

TABLE 1 Mass spectra data

Mass spectra	*m*/*z* value for the molecular ion	Base value	Cl or Br present?	Odd number of N atoms?	Suspected organic compound
1					
2					
3					
4					
5					
6	103	76	No	Yes	Benzonitrile
7					
8					

3 For each of the infrared spectra, use the infrared data table in the QCAA Chemistry formula and data book to match the correct wavelength of a band with the presence or absence of a functional group, and record your results in Table 2.

TABLE 2 Infrared spectra data

Infrared spectra	Wavelength or band relied on for assignment	Presence of which functional group?	Bands not observed in these wavelengths	Absence of which functional group?
1				
2				
3				
4				
5				
6	3177 and 3369	Alcohol	3326	Carboxylic acid
7				
8				

4 Match the correct mass spectra with the correct infrared spectra and determine the correct organic compounds. Record your results in Table 3 below.

Hint: One match and two organic compounds have already been identified in the table below.

TABLE 3 Identification of organic compounds

Mass spectra	Infrared spectra	Organic compound
1		Benzoic acid
2		Benzyl bromide
3		
4	8	
5		
6	3	Benzonitrile
7		Benzamide
8		

Discussion

1 Evaluate your answers.

Haber process simulation using Wolfram

Unit 4, Topic 2: Simulations of the Haber process could be used.

Source: *Chemistry 2019 v1.3 General Senior Syllabus* © Queensland Curriculum & Assessment Authority

Aim

To investigate the effect of pressure and temperature on the equilibrium concentrations of the Haber process reaction mixture.

Materials

- Computer

Method and Results

Part A: Pre-lab

1 The simulation for this activity is, Chemical equilibrium in the Haber Process by Wolfram. Firstly, go to http://demonstrations.wolfram.com/ChemicalEquilibriumInTheHaberProcess/ and download the program 'ChemicalEquilibriumInTheHaberProcess.cdf' (97 kB). Secondly, to use this simulation you will need to download the 1.5 MB downloader which, when executed, will download the 1 GB 'CDF player'. Do this before the lesson begins because it takes 20 minutes.

2 Deduce the equilibrium expression for the Haber process, assuming all components are in the gas phase.

____

Part B: Effect of temperature

3 Set the pressure to 200 bar (20 000 kPa) and a temperature of 600 K by using the sliders at the top. Add 1 mol of each substance by using the sliders at the top. Use the sliders to increase and decrease the temperature, and record the equilibrium amounts in Table 1 below. Nitrogen has already been added to the table as 0.82 mol.

TABLE 1 Equilibrium amounts as a function of temperature

Temperature (K)	Amount of substance at equilibrium (mol)		
	N_2	H_2	NH_3
400			
450			
500			
550			
600	0.82		
650			
700			
750			

a Describe the effect of increasing the temperature on the equilibrium mixture.

b Explain the effect of temperature on the position of equilibrium.

c Propose how increasing temperature for an exothermic reaction is consistent with Le Châtelier's principle.

Part C: Effect of pressure

4 Leave the pressure at 200 bar (20 000 kPa), and the amounts of the three reactants at 1 mol each. Reset the temperature to 600 K. The amount of N_2 at equilibrium is already in Table 2 below. Use the sliders to increase the pressure to 250 bar (25 000 kPa) and record the equilibrium amounts of the three components (in mol) in Table 2. Reduce the pressure and record the amounts.

TABLE 2 Equilibrium amounts as a function of pressure

Pressure (bar) (× 100 kPa)	Amount of substance at equilibrium (mol)		
	N_2	H_2	NH_3
50			
100			
150			
200	0.82		
250			

a Describe the effect of increasing the pressure on the equilibrium mixture.

b Explain the effect of pressure on the position of equilibrium.

c Propose how increasing pressure for an exothermic reaction is consistent with Le Châtelier's principle.

Part D: Effect of concentration

5 Reset the pressure to 200 bar (20 000 kPa), and the amounts of the three reactants to 1 mol each. Ensure the temperature is still at 600 K. Use sliders to add additional moles of nitrogen, hydrogen and ammonia at constant pressure of 250 bar and constant temperature (600 K) and observe how they change equilibrium, recording your results in Tables 3 to 5.

TABLE 3 Equilibrium amounts as a function of N_2

Amount of N_2 (mol)	Amount of substance at equilibrium (mol)		
	N_2	H_2	NH_3
0.0			
0.5			
1.0	0.82		
1.5			
2.0			

a Describe the effect of increasing N_2 concentration.

TABLE 4 Equilibrium amounts as a function of H_2

Amount of H_2 (mol)	Amount of substance at equilibrium (mol)		
	N_2	H_2	NH_3
0.0			
0.5			
1.0	0.82		
1.5			
2.0			

b Describe the effect of increasing H_2 concentration.

____

____

____

TABLE 5 Equilibrium amounts as a function of NH_3

Amount of NH_3 (mol)	Amount of substance at equilibrium (mol)		
	N_2	H_2	NH_3
1.0	0.82		
1.5			
2.0			
2.5			
3.0			

c Describe the effect of increasing NH_3 concentration.

____

____

____

Discussion

1 Evaluate the claim:

Le Châtelier's principle predicts that when moles of nitrogen or hydrogen are added, reaction shifts to the right, whereas adding ammonia shifts the reaction to the left.

In your response, show that when the nitrogen/hydrogen ratio is sufficiently high, adding nitrogen shifts reaction to the left (i.e. adding nitrogen increases the amount of hydrogen, contrary to Le Châtelier's principle). (**Hint:** Adding nitrogen when the N/H ratio is high decreases the hydrogen mole fraction.)

____

____

____

____

____

____

____

____

____

Video simulation of the contact process

Unit 4, Topic 2: Simulations of contact process could be used.

Source: *Chemistry 2019 v1.3 General Senior Syllabus* © Queensland Curriculum & Assessment Authority

Aim

To understand the formation of sulfuric acid through the contact process.

Materials

- Computer

Method

1 The simulations for this activity are 'Dynamic science' and 'FuseSchool' videos. Use these two resources to gain a better understanding of the contact process: http://www.dynamicscience.com.au/tester/solutions1/chemistry/sulfuricacid.html and https://www.youtube.com/watch?v=xjLUJ-7m5v8.

Results

Use the simulations online to answer questions on the contact process.

1 Write the balanced chemical reactions for the three different stages of the contact process.

Stage one: making sulfur dioxide

Stage two: making sulfur trioxide

Stage three: making sulfuric acid

2 Research the different uses of sulfuric acid.

Answers

Chapter 1

DATA DRILL 1

1 a Control sample

b $MnO_4^-(aq) + 8H^+(aq) + 5e^- \rightarrow$
$Mn^{2+}(aq) + 4H_2O(l)$

c

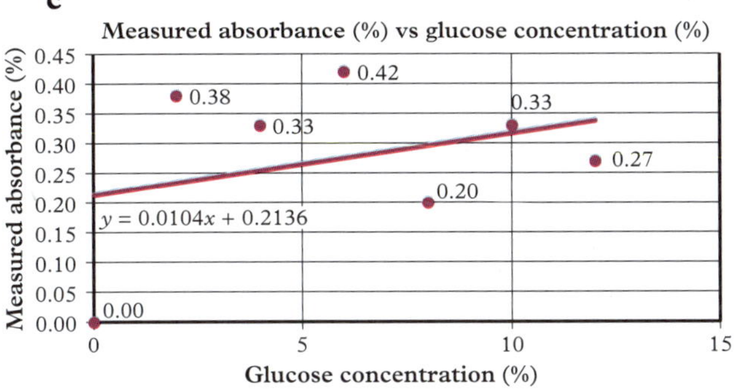

Slightly positive linear relationship, if plotted in Excel. Relationship is difficult to determine, if plotted by hand, because of the scatter of data.

EXPERIMENT EXPLORER 1

1 Student answers will vary; a sample response is provided below.

Aim: To measure the electrical conductivity of acid solutions by using a multimeter water tester to determine their strength in solution.

Hypothesis: Solutions with low conductivity do not readily ionise in solution and are weak acids. Solutions with high conductivity dissociate into ions and are strong acids.

Materials:

- Digital multimeter water tester
- Deionised water (for rinsing)
- Small beaker(s)
- Marker pens
- Various 0.2 M solutions of acids (e.g. HNO_3, H_2SO_4, CH_3COOH, HCl, citric acid, benzoic acid, deionised water, tap water etc.)
- Paper or insulating mat (to keep laboratory benches clean)
- Paper towel (for clean-up)
- Plastic container (for waste chemicals)

Method:

1 Safely collect laboratory equipment and materials and assemble on the bench. Handle glass apparatus with care to prevent cuts or skin abrasions.

2 Pour a small amount of each acidic solution into a small beaker. Label with a marker.

3 Place the dry digital multimeter water tester electrode into one of the labelled beakers and take a direct reading of the conductivity of that substance. Record the result in a table.

4 Rinse the multimeter water tester electrode with deionised water and dry with a tissue.

5 Repeat Steps 3 and 4 above until all of the acidic solutions have been measured and recorded.

6 When finished, tip the contents of the labelled beakers into a plastic container for waste. Clean up the bench.

Results:

Acid	Measured conductivity (mS cm^{-1})
Deionised water	0.05
Tap water	0.63
Nitric acid	350
Hydrochloric acid	700
Sulfuric acid	850
Acetic acid	350
Citric acid	200
Benzoic acid	500

Results can be communicated by a scientific poster, a laboratory report or an oral presentation.

2 A sugar solution could be used as a control in this experiment. A glucose molecule ($C_6H_{12}O_6$) is a covalently bonded molecule and therefore does not form ions in solution and will not conduct electricity.

RESEARCH REVIEW 1

Student answers will vary depending on each student's resources. Guidance is provided here.

Resources should be based on a molecular engineering process for one of the industries mentioned in the question and cited using American Psychological Association (APA) style (6th edition) (or other referencing style) as practice for the student experiment and/or poster presentation.

Credible resources include peer-reviewed journals, government or organisation websites, and company or university websites that are unbiased; they are written with purpose and backed by evidence or supporting documentation (e.g. graphs, tables, charts and illustrations) relevant to the topic.

Non-credible resources include those that use all capital letters, usually have the suffix 'lo' or '.com.co', have sensationalist headlines and/or photos, have memes, and have an amateurish design.

UNIT 3 WORD WIZARD

ENTHALPY	the energy stored within chemical substances, referred to as its chemical energy or heat content
DYNAMIC EQUILIBRIUM	the state a reaction reaches when the rates of the forward and reverse reactions are equal
MONOPROTIC ACID	an acid that can donate one hydrogen ion per molecule
ELECTRICAL CONDUCTIVITY	the degree to which a material conducts an electric current
pK_a	a measure of acid strength; the negative common logarithm (to base 10) of the acid dissociation constant
STRONG BASE	a base that completely ionises in water
END POINT	the point in a titration when the indicator changes colour
TITRATION	the addition of a solution of known concentration to a known volume of another solution of unknown concentration until the reaction reaches neutralisation
OXIDATION	a loss of electrons from one atom to another atom
ELECTRO-NEGATIVITY	the attraction between a positively charged nucleus and the negatively charged electrons of a neighbouring atom
OXIDATION NUMBER	the number of electrons gained or lost by an atom
HALF-EQUATION	an equation that represents either an oxidation or a reduction half of a chemical equation; it includes electrons to demonstrate electron transfer
GALVANIC CELL	an electrochemical cell in which the reduction and oxidation half-equations are separated and connected through a circuit to generate electricity
CATHODE	the positively charged electrode, where reduction occurs
FUEL CELL	a galvanic cell that produces electricity by using a constant supply of reactants (often hydrogen and oxygen) and inert electrodes that do not break down
ELECTROLYSIS	the process by which electrical energy is passed into a cell, using a power source, resulting in the reversal of spontaneous redox reactions
REDUCING AGENT	a reactant that causes another reactant to gain electrons and be reduced and is itself oxidised

Chapter 2

DATA DRILL 2

1 **a** **i** 0.22

ii 0.24

b The two values of calculated K_c in 1ai and 1aii are almost the same because the temperature of the system was not changed.

EXPERIMENT EXPLORER 2

1 Concentration of Cl^- increases, equilibrium shifts forward, and solution turns blue due to chloro cobalt(II) complex.

2 Endothermic direction favoured with heat, equilibrium shifts forward, and solution turns blue.

3 Exothermic direction favoured with ice bath, equilibrium shifts backward, forming more pink hydrated complex.

RESEARCH REVIEW 2

1 Student answers will vary depending on each student's resources. Students need to use the guidelines provided in Research review 2. An example answer is provided below.

In-text citation: (Kondo et al., 2006)

Reference list: Kondo, S., Takizawa, K., Takahashi A. and Tokuhashi, K., 2006, Extended Le Chatelier's formula for carbon dioxide dilution effect on flammability limits, Journal of Hazardous Materials, 138, 1, 1–8.

EXAM EXCELLENCE 2

1 C **2** C **3** A **4** B **5** C

6 **a** Burning fossil fuels.

b Equation 1: Carbon dioxide in the air dissolves in seawater to form carbonic acid. As the concentration of carbon dioxide increases, the equilibrium shifts forward and more carbon dioxide dissolves.

Equation 2: The increased carbon dioxide in the air eventually becomes incorporated into calcium carbonate in the form of limestone deposits and shells on the sea floor.

7 a $110\ M^{-1}$

b Not at equilibrium. More N_2O_4 must form.

8

Change to the system	Net shift	Effect on the number of moles of H_2
Addition of nitrogen	No effect	No effect
Decrease in pressure	Left	Increase
Increase in temperature	Left	Increase
Volume halved	Right	Decrease
Methanol removed	Right	Decrease

9

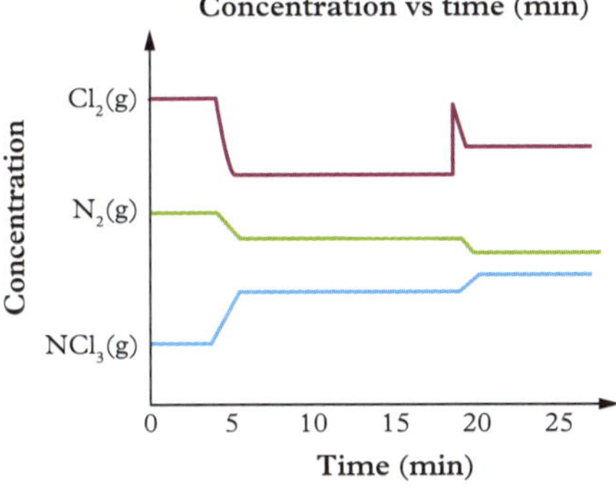

10 a $2A(g) + B(g) \rightleftharpoons C(g) + 3D(g)$

b Very low ratio; mostly products in the equilibrium mixture (large K_c).

Chapter 3

DATA DRILL 3

1 a Positive linear relationship. For example, in 1990 the atmospheric CO_2 level was 350 ppm and increased to 375 ppm in 2005.

b Positive linear relationship. For example, in 1990 the seawater CO_2 level was 325 µatm and increased to 350 µatm in 2004.

c Negative linear relationship. For example, in 1990 the pH of seawater was about 8.12 and decreased to about 8.08 in 2007. The overall trend in the graph is that as the levels of CO_2 increase in the atmosphere and ocean, the pH of the seawater decreases and becomes more acidic.

EXPERIMENT EXPLORER 3

1 Student answers will vary; a sample response is provided below.

Aim: To measure the pH of household substances by using a pH meter to classify them as acids, bases or neutral substances.

Hypothesis: Substances with low pH are acidic, substances with high pH are basic, and substances with a mid-range pH are neutral.

Materials:

- Digital pH meter
- Tissues
- Deionised water (for rinsing)
- Small beaker(s)
- Small test tubes
- Marker pens
- Test-tube rack
- Household substances (e.g. water, milk, lemonade, lemon juice, vinegar, shampoo, bicarbonate of soda, bathroom or surface cleaners etc.)
- Paper or insulating mat
- Paper towel
- Plastic waste container

Method:

1 Safely collect laboratory equipment and materials and assemble on the bench. Handle glass apparatus with care to prevent cuts or skin abrasions.

2 Pour a small amount of each household substance (if a liquid) into a test tube. Label with a marker and place in the test-tube rack.

3 If the household substance is a solid or viscous (thick) liquid, dissolve a small amount in a test tube with deionised water, label with a marker, and set aside in the test-tube rack.

4 Place the dry pH meter electrode into one of the labelled test tubes and take a direct reading of the pH of that substance. Record the result in a table.

5 Rinse the pH meter electrode with deionised water and dry with a tissue.

6 Repeat Steps 4 and 5 above until all of the household substances have been measured and recorded in a table.

7 When finished, tip the contents of the labelled test tubes into a plastic container as waste. Clean up the bench.

Results:

Household substance	Measured pH	Acid/base/neutral
Water	7.0	Neutral
Vinegar	2.8	Weak acid
Bicarbonate of soda	9.1	Weak base
Lemonade	3.2	Weak acid
Surface cleaner (alkaline)	13.8	Strong base
Lemon juice	2.4	Weak acid
Surface cleaner (acidic)	2.0	Strong acid

Results can be communicated by a scientific poster, a laboratory report or an oral presentation.

RESEARCH REVIEW 3

1 Student answers will vary depending on each student's resources. Guidance is provided below.

Resources should be based on the pH scale and/or classifying substances based on the pH scale, and cited using APA style (6th edition) (or other referencing style) as practice for the student experiment and/or poster presentation.

For guidance on credible and non-credible resources, refer to Research review 1 answers.

EXAM EXCELLENCE 3

1 A **2** D **3** D **4** A **5** B

6 a $H_2CrO_4(aq) + H_2O(l) \rightarrow HCrO_4^-(aq) + H_3O^+(aq)$

$HCrO_4^-(aq) + H_2O(l) \rightleftharpoons CrO_4^{2-}(aq) + H_3O^+(aq)$

Note: Second ionisation occurs less often.

b $PH_3(aq) + H_2O(l) \rightleftharpoons PH_4^+(aq) + OH^-(aq)$

7 a $0.004\ mol\ L^{-1}$

b 14.3

8 a, b $HBr(aq) + H_2O(l) \rightarrow Br^-(aq) + H_3O^+(aq)$

acid — base — conjugate base — conjugate acid

$HOI(aq) + H_2O(l) \rightleftharpoons OI^-(aq) + H_3O^+(aq)$

acid — base — conjugate base — conjugate acid

9 If the soil is acidic, the reaction will consume more $HPO_4^{2-}(aq)$ and the equilibrium shifts backward, resulting in more $H_2PO_4^-(aq)$ present in the soil.

10 a $1 \times 10^{-4}\ mol\ L^{-1}$

b $HCOOH(aq)_3 + H_2O(l) \rightleftharpoons H_3O^+(aq) + HCOO^-(aq)$

Chapter 4

DATA DRILL 4

1 a

Acid	Condensed formula	Molar mass	pk_a
Formic acid	$HCOOH$	46	3.75
Acetic acid	CH_3COOH	60	4.76
Propanoic acid	CH_3CH_2COOH	74	4.87
Butanoic acid	$CH_3(CH_2)_2COOH$	88	4.83
Pentanoic acid	$CH_3(CH_2)_3COOH$	102	4.83
Hexanoic acid	$CH_3(CH_2)_4COOH$	116	4.85
Heptanoic acid	$CH_3(CH_2)_5COOH$	130	4.89
Octanoic acid	$CH_3(CH_2)_6COOH$	144	4.89
Nonanoic acid	$CH_3(CH_2)_7COOH$	158	4.96

b

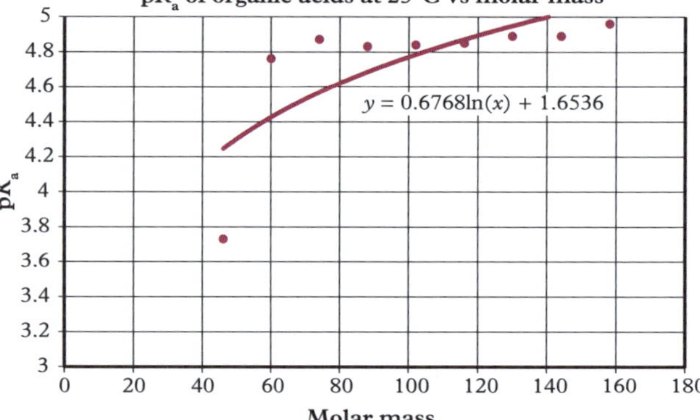

Positive logarithmic relationship.

c Decanoic acid has a molar mass of 172, so from the graph, pK_a is predicted to be very close to 5 (trendline equation on the graph gives 5.14).

EXPERIMENT EXPLORER 4

1 a Phenol red

b Cresolphthalein (meta)

RESEARCH REVIEW 4

Student answers will vary depending on each student's question. Guidance is provided below.

Student questions should consider the following:

- the definition of a 'superacid' and its properties
- examples of their uses, including breaking down petroleum and other hydrocarbons.

EXAM EXCELLENCE 4

1 B 2 B 3 B 4 A 5 A

6 a $HOCl(aq) + H_2O(l) \rightleftharpoons OCl^-(aq) + H_3O^+(aq)$

 b 3.88

 c $2.65 \times 10^{-2}\%$ (or 0.03%)

7 9.3×10^{-2} M

8 3.2×10^{-8}

9 $HIn^-(aq) + H^+(aq) \rightleftharpoons H_2In(aq)$

yellow acid red

weak base conjugate acid

10 6.32×10^{-3} M

EXPERIMENT EXPLORER 5

1

Hazard	What are the risks?	What is the level of risk? (high/ medium/low)	What are the controls?
White tile/glassware/ pipettes/burette	May cause cuts, abrasions and/or lacerations if not handled correctly.	Low	Wear personal protective equipment (PPE). Handle with care. Do not use if cracked.
Retort stand and boss head and clamp	Centre of mass of supported object is often high, and the stand may topple over. May cause cuts, abrasions and/or lacerations if not handled correctly.	Low	Wear PPE. Handle with care.
Acid solution (approx. 1 M)	May cause irritation to eyes, lungs and skin at high concentrations. Avoid inhalation of vapour.	Low	Wear PPE. Work in a well-ventilated area.
Base solution (approx. 1 M)	May cause irritation to eyes, lungs and skin at high concentrations. Avoid inhalation of vapour.	Low	Wear PPE. Work in a well-ventilated area.
Salt solution (product of the neutralisation reaction in the experiment)	Not classified as hazardous (usually). May cause irritation to eyes if not handled correctly.	Low	Wear PPE.
Phenolphthalein solution (0.1% w/w in ethanol)	Danger! Highly flammable liquid and vapour. Causes serious eye irritation. Carcinogenic. Suspected of causing genetic defects. Suspected of damaging fertility. Do not use near ignition sources. Prolonged contact with skin causes irritation.	High	Wear PPE. Work in a well-ventilated area. Do not use near ignition sources.

RESEARCH REVIEW 5

Student posters will vary considerably. Students should follow the guidelines listed in the assessment task.

EXAM EXCELLENCE 5

1 B 2 B 3 D 4 D 5 B

Chapter 5

DATA DRILL 5

1 Strong acid and strong base. End point at 24 mL and equivalence point at 22 mL. Volume required is 22 mL.

2 Phenolphthalein, thymol blue, cresol red or thymolphthalein. These indicators will change colour at the equivalence point at approximately pH = 7.8.

6 a $H_2SO_4(aq) + 2KOH(aq) \rightarrow K_2SO_4(aq) + 2H_2O(l)$

 b 9.997 mL

 c 0.00406 mol

 d 0.00203 mol

7 a $H_2C_2O_4(aq) + 2NaOH(aq) \rightarrow Na_2C_2O_4(aq) + 2H_2O(l)$

 b 0.224 M

8 a Thymol blue, cresol red or thymolphthalein. These indicators will change colour at the equivalence point at approximately pH = 8.3.

b Weak acid, $K_a = 7.94 \times 10^{-5}$

9 a The pH at the equivalence point of Titration A would be pH = 7 (strong acid/strong base). The pH at the equivalence point of Titration B would be pH > 7 (weak acid/strong base).

b A weak acid/strong base forms a basic salt:

$2NaOH(aq) + H_2CO_3(aq) \rightleftharpoons Na_2CO_3(aq) + 2H_2O(l)$

At the equivalence point, the dissociation of $H_2CO_3(aq)$ forms $CO_3^{2-}(aq)$ ions, which then react with water to form $HCO_3^-(aq)$ (weak base), which is expected to have a pH > 7:

$CO_3^{2-}(aq) + H_2O(l) \rightleftharpoons HCO_3^-(aq) + OH^-(aq)$

10 a $HCl(aq) + NH_3(aq) \rightarrow NH_4Cl(aq)$

b 21.23 mL

c 2.166×10^{-3} mol

d 2.166×10^{-3} mol

e 0.11 M (0.1083 M)

Chapter 6

DATA DRILL 6

1 a Positive linear relationship. Gradient = 0.0198

Equation: BAC = 0.0198 × number of drinks

b 0.198

EXPERIMENT EXPLORER 6

1 a Beaker 1: No reaction.

Beaker 2: Zinc deposited on the magnesium strip.

Beaker 3: Copper deposited on the magnesium strip.

Beaker 4: Silver deposited on the magnesium strip.

b Beaker 1: No reaction.

Beaker 2:

$Mg(s) \rightarrow Mg^{2+}(aq) + 2e^-$ oxidation

$Zn^{2+}(aq) + 2e^- \rightarrow Zn(s)$ reduction

Beaker 3:

$Mg(s) \rightarrow Mg^{2+}(aq) + 2e^-$ oxidation

$Cu^{2+}(aq) + 2e^- \rightarrow Cu(s)$ reduction

Beaker 4:

$Mg(s) \rightarrow Mg^{2+}(aq) + 2e^-$ oxidation

$2Ag^+(aq) + 2e^- \rightarrow 2Ag(s)$ reduction

c Only a reaction in Beaker 4, with silver deposited on the copper strip:

$Cu(s) \rightarrow Cu^{2+}(aq) + 2e^-$ oxidation

$2Ag^+(aq) + 2e^- \rightarrow 2Ag(s)$ reduction

This is due to copper metal being more reactive than silver and less reactive than magnesium and zinc in the metal reactivity series.

RESEARCH REVIEW 6

Student answers will vary depending on each student's question. Guidance is provided below.

Student questions should consider the following:

- the types of iron ore used for steel manufacture
- the raw materials and oxidation and reduction reactions used for extracting molten iron from ores in blast furnace processes.
- the side oxidation and reduction reactions for removal of iron impurities (e.g. 'slag')
- the types of steel that can be produced according to the amount of carbon present.

EXAM EXCELLENCE 6

1 A 2 D 3 A 4 B 5 C

6
S	0
SO_2	+4
SO_3	+6
SO_4^{2-}	+6
H_2S	−2

7 a Metal B is more reactive. In Beaker 1, metal A is lower in the reactivity series than the solution of the metal ions (B^+) that it is placed in; no reaction will occur. In Beaker 2, metal B is higher in the reactivity series than the solution of the metal ions (A^+) that it is placed in. Because of the difference in reactivity, metal B slowly corrodes and loses electrons (forming ions) in the aqueous solution. The metal ions (A^+) from the solution accept or gain those electrons and form a solid coating on metal B.

b Beaker 1: $A(s) \rightarrow A(s)$ and $B^+(aq) \rightarrow B^+(aq)$ (no reaction)

Beaker 2: $B(s) \rightarrow B^+(aq) + e^-$ (oxidation half-equation)

$A^+(aq) + e^- \rightarrow A(s)$ (reduction half-equation)

$A^+(aq)$ is the species causing reduction and is the strongest oxidant.

8 a Oxidant is $Cr_2O_7^{2-}(aq)$ and reductant is NO(g).

b $Cr_2O_7^{2-}(aq) + 14H^+(aq) + 6e^- \rightarrow 2Cr^{3+}(aq) + 7H_2O(l)$

$NO(g) + 2H_2O(l) \rightarrow NO_3^-(aq) + 4H^+(aq) + 3e^-$

9 A reaction is defined as a redox reaction if one reactant undergoes oxidation (loss of electrons) and the other reactant undergoes reduction (gain of electrons) at the same time.

For example: $Mg(s) + Cl_2(g) \rightarrow MgCl_2(s)$

The oxidation half-equation is $Mg(s) \rightarrow Mg^{2+}(aq) + 2e^-$ (the oxidation number of Mg increases from 0 to +2).

The reduction half-equation is $Cl_2(g) + 2e^- \rightarrow 2Cl^-(aq)$ (the oxidation number of Cl decreases from 0 to −1).

10 Oxidation numbers are above the equations.

a $\overset{0}{2Na(s)} + \overset{0}{Cl_2(g)} \rightarrow \overset{+1\,-1}{2NaCl(s)}$

Redox reaction: oxidant is $Cl_2(g)$ and reductant is Na(s).

b $\overset{+2\,-2\,+1}{Ca(OH)_2(aq)} + \overset{+1\,+5\,-2}{2HNO_3(aq)} \rightarrow$

$\overset{+2\,+5\,-2}{Ca(NO_3)_2(aq)} + \overset{+1\,-2}{2H_2O(l)}$

No oxidant or reductant (equation is an acid–base reaction).

c $\overset{+1\,+5\,-2}{AgNO_3(aq)} + \overset{+1\,-1}{NaCl(aq)} \rightarrow$

$\overset{+1\,-1}{AgCl(s)} + \overset{+1\,+5\,-2}{NaNO_3(aq)}$

No oxidant or reductant (equation is a precipitation reaction).

d $\overset{+2\,+6\,-2}{CuSO_4(aq)} + \overset{0}{Zn(s)} \rightarrow$

$\overset{0}{Cu(s)} + \overset{+2\,+6\,-2}{ZnSO_4(aq)}$

Redox reaction: oxidant is $Cu^{2+}(aq)$ and reductant is Zn(s).

Chapter 7

DATA DRILL 7

1 a Beaker 1: $Zn(s) \rightarrow Zn^{2+}(aq) + 2e^-$ oxidation

Beaker 2: $Cu^{2+}(aq) + 2e^- \rightarrow Cu(s)$ reduction

b

Temp (°C)	Trial 1 voltage (V)	Trial 2 voltage (V)	Trial 3 voltage (V)	Trial 4 voltage (V)	Trial 5 voltage (V)	Average voltage (V)
0	0.91	0.90	0.91	0.87	0.89	0.90
3	0.91	0.94	0.90	0.95	0.93	0.93
15	0.83	0.85	0.86	0.83	0.86	0.85
22	0.84	0.85	0.82	0.86	0.85	0.84
54	0.85	0.82	0.78	0.85	0.84	0.83

c

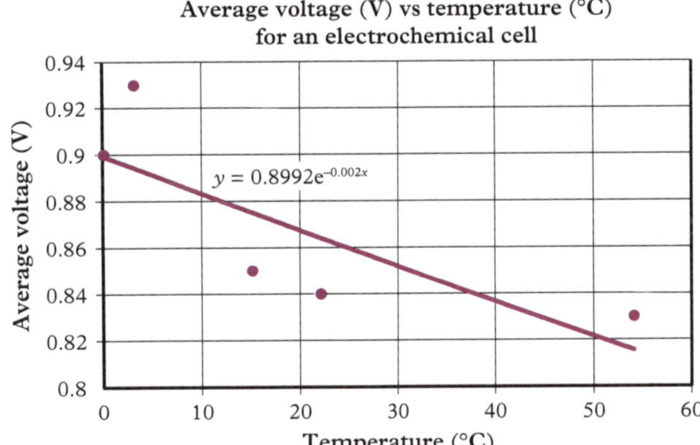

Positive exponential relationship.

d 0.86 V (0.8553 V using an Excel trendline)

EXPERIMENT EXPLORER 7

1 a

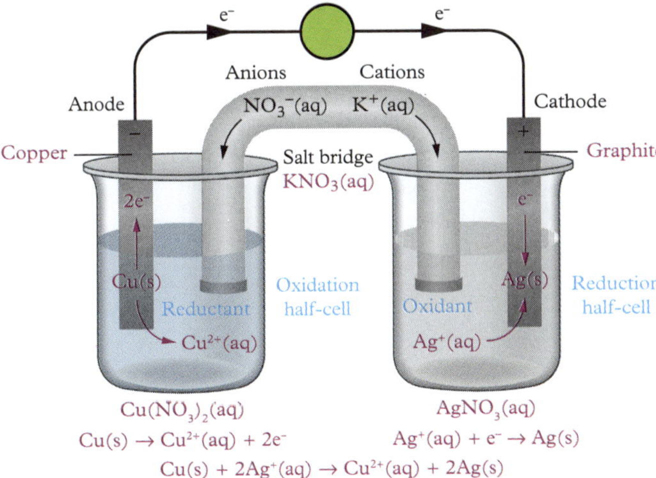

EMF = +0.46 V

RESEARCH REVIEW 7

1 Research may vary, but the following points need to be addressed. Claim b is the most credible claim.

Claim a: There are six types of fuel cells, not one. Fuel cells also have a wide variety of usages.

Claim b: Space shuttles have three fuel cells that are used to power the shuttles. Without fuel cells, the shuttles would not be able to transport people to space.

EXAM EXCELLENCE 7

1 C   2 B   3 A   4 D   5 A

6 a $2Cl^-(aq) \rightarrow Cl_2(g) + 2e^-$ oxidation

$Au^{3+}(aq) + 3e^- \rightarrow Au(s)$ reduction

Overall:

$6Cl^-(aq) + 2Au^{3+}(aq) \rightarrow 3Cl_2(g) + 2Au(s)$

b $Au^{3+}(aq)$

c c +1.50 V

7 a Yes

b No

8 a No

b Yes

9 a $Sn(s) \rightarrow Sn^{2+}(aq) + 2e^-$ oxidation

$Cr_2O_7^{2-}(aq) + 14H^+(aq) + 6e^- \rightarrow 2Cr^{3+}(aq) + 7H_2O(l)$ reduction

Overall: $3Sn(s) + Cr_2O_7^{2-}(aq) + 14H^+(aq) \rightarrow 3Sn^{2+}(aq) + 2Cr^{3+}(aq) + 7H_2O(l)$

b 1.50 V

10 a Electrode X(s)

b $X(s) \rightarrow X^{2+}(aq) + 2e^-$ oxidation

$2Ag^+(aq) + 2e^- \rightarrow 2Ag(s)$ reduction

Overall: $X(s) + 2Ag^+(aq) \rightarrow X^{2+}(aq) + 2Ag(s)$

c Anode is X(s).

d Cathode is Ag(s).

e Towards Ag(s).

Chapter 8

DATA DRILL 8

1 a $Cu(s) \rightarrow Cu^{2+}(aq) + 2e^-$ oxidation, at positive anode

$Cu^{2+}(aq) + 2e^- \rightarrow Cu(s)$ reduction, at negative cathode

b Positive linear relationship

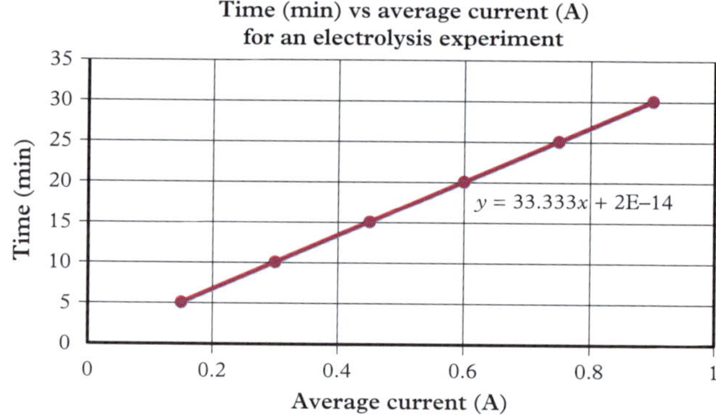

EXPERIMENT EXPLORER 8

1

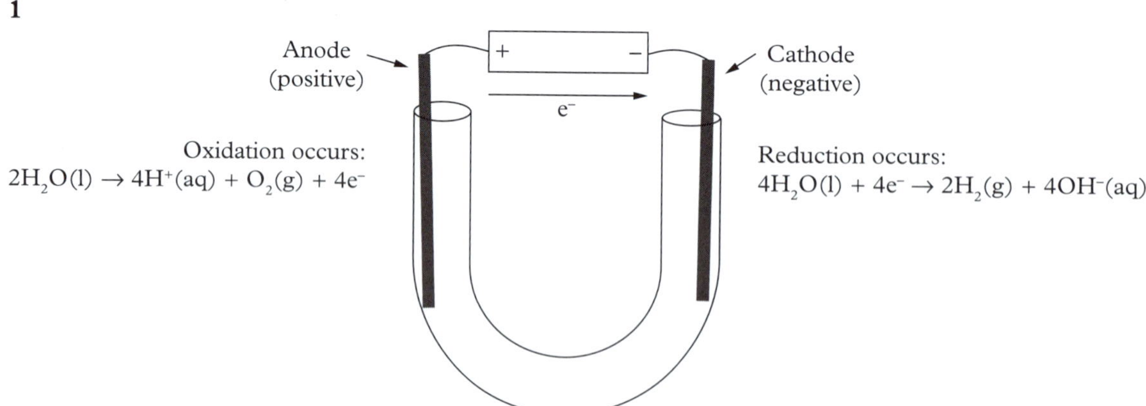

Overall: $6H_2O(l) \rightarrow 2H_2(g) + O_2(g) + 4H^+(aq) + 4OH^-(aq)$ $E^\circ = -2.06$ V

Species present: $Na^+(aq)$, $SO_4^{2-}(aq)$, $H_2O(l)$, $H^+(aq)$, $OH^-(aq)$, $H_2(g)$, $O_2(g)$

Note: The Na^+ ion is difficult to reduce because its metal is reactive.

RESEARCH REVIEW 8

Student answers will vary depending on each student's resources. Guidance is provided below.

Resources should be based on the use of electrolysis reactions from one of the applications mentioned in the question and cited using APA style (6th edition) (or other referencing style) as practice for the student experiment and/or poster presentation.

For guidance on credible and non-credible resources, refer to Research review 1 answers.

EXAM EXCELLENCE 8

1 D **2** D **3** C **4** B **5** A

6 a Cell A: Copper refinement or extraction of copper metal. Cell B: Electroplating for decorative effect.

b The colour of the blue solution remains the same because the copper ions are being deposited on the bracelet as Cu(s) is being replaced in solution by the copper electrode.

c The sludge on the bottom could contain precious metals like silver and gold.

7 a Carbon or graphite.

b $2Br^-(aq) \rightarrow Br_2(g) + 2e^-$

$4H_2O(l) + 4e^- \rightarrow 2H_2(g) + 4OH^-(aq)$

$4Br^-(aq) + 4H_2O(l) \rightarrow$
$2Br_2(g) + 2H_2(g) + 4OH^-(aq)$

8 a $2H_2O(l) \rightarrow 4H^+(aq) + O_2(g) + 4e^-$

b Decreased pH.

9 a Anode: $PbSO_4(aq) + 2H_2O(l) \rightarrow$
$PbO_2(s) + SO_4^{2-}(aq) + 4H^+(aq) + 2e^-$

Cathode: $PbSO_4(aq) + 2e^- \rightarrow Pb(s) + SO_4^{2-}(aq)$

b Advantages: rechargeable, delivers large amount of energy. Disadvantages: bulky size, heavy to carry, acid spill risk, toxic components.

10 a Allows positive cations to migrate to the cathode half-cell.

b Y electrode because chloride ions are oxidised at electrode Y.

c Gas A is $H_2(g)$, Gas B is $Cl_2(g)$ and Compound C is NaOH(aq).

d Anode (oxidation): $2Cl^-(aq) \rightarrow$
$Cl_2(g) + 2e^-$

Cathode (reduction): $2H_2O(l) + 2e^- \rightarrow$
$H_2(g) + 2OH^-(aq)$

Overall: $2H_2O(l) + 2Cl^-(aq) \rightarrow$
$H_2(g) + 2OH^-(aq) + Cl_2(g)$

Unit 3 Practice assessment

DATA TEST

Dataset 1

Item 1:

$HCl(aq) + NaOH(aq) \rightarrow NaCl(aq) + H_2O(l)$

Item 2:

11.48 mL

Item 3:

The student's first titre is not concordant with the rest of their recorded titres (i.e. random error).

Item 4:

0.0861 M

Item 5:

344.4 g

Dataset 2

Item 6:

2.5

Item 7:

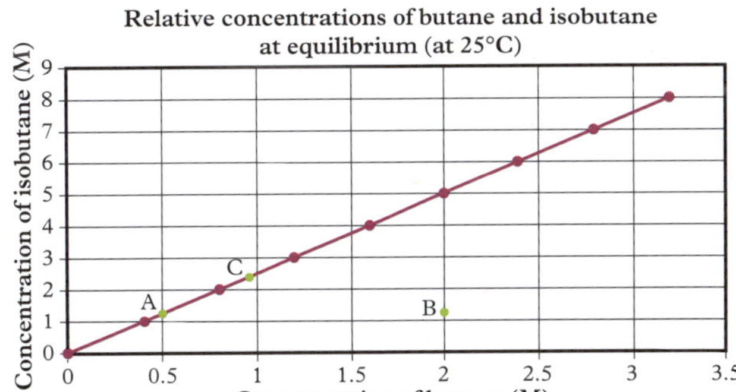

Item 8:

At point B, Q would be less than K because more butane was added to the system. Adding more reactant causes a net forward reaction, increasing the ratio of isobutane to butane.

Item 9:

As equilibrium is re-established, each mole of butane consumed produces one mole of isobutane.

STUDENT EXPERIMENT

Student answers will vary based on the choice of modification, but students should make sure their experiment still reflects the concept of 'measuring pH'. Below is a checklist that each student should complete as they work through their student experiment.

- Consider whether the aim needs to be changed after the modification.
- Construct a research question.
- Research relevant literature if required for the modification.
- Complete a risk assessment for the new experiment and get it signed by a teacher.
- Complete the experiment to know it works.
- Collect enough data to answer the research question.
- Present the data in an appropriate scientific genre.
- Analyse any trends and limitations of the dataset.
- Draw conclusions of the new experiment and how it improves the experiment.

RESEARCH INVESTIGATION

Student answers will vary depending on each student's research question and resources.

A sample research question is: 'How does ocean acidification impact the coastal society of Mackay?'

Resources should include information on Mackay's coastal society and evidence of ocean acidification in the area.

UNIT 4 WORD WIZARD

HYDROCARBON	an organic compound consisting of only carbon and hydrogen atoms
KETONE	a class of organic compound that has a carbonyl group on a carbon within the main chain
AMIDE	a class of organic compound that contains amine and carbonyl functional groups adjacent to each other
HALOALKANE	a class of organic compound that contains a halogen substituent
MONOMER	a single unit within a polymer
ESTERIFICATION	a condensation reaction between a carboxylic acid and alcohol that generates an ester
POLYSACCHARIDE	a complex sugar consisting of multiple sugar monomers bonded together
PEPTIDE BOND	the bond joining amino acid monomers together, between the carboxyl and amine groups of adjacent amino acids
MASS SPECTROMETRY	a technique used to determine the molecular weight of a compound
INFRARED RADIATION	electromagnetic radiation in the region between visible light and microwave radiation
HABER PROCESS	a nitrogen fixation process to produce ammonia
CONTACT PROCESS	the production of very concentrated sulfuric acid
RENEWABLE	replaceable at a rate equal to or greater than the rate of use, over an indefinite period
CATALYST	a substance that increases the rate of a reaction without itself being consumed in the reaction
SUPERCRITICAL FLUID	a substance at a temperature and pressure beyond its critical point, where the substance has properties of both a gas and liquid
BIODEGRADATION	the breakdown of a substance, such as plastic, by microorganisms
MOLECULAR MANUFACTURING	the atomically precise placement of atoms or molecules in order to build larger molecular assemblies or molecular-based machines

Chapter 9

RESEARCH REVIEW 9

Student research and notes will vary depending on each student's selected application. Students need to have credible resources to formulate their speech. Guidance on speeches includes:

- use visual aids (PowerPoint, props etc.).
- tell a compelling story with a beginning, middle and end.
- engage the audience and ask questions.
- practise the speech many times out loud.
- have prompts in the presentation or on cue cards.

- present confidently; people want to hear what you have to say.
- avoid reading off notes.
- look past people if you are feeling nervous.

EXAM EXCELLENCE 9

1 C **2** D **3** D **4** D **5** B

6 a Alcohols form hydrogen bonds between molecules and hence have stronger intermolecular forces and higher boiling points than those of alkanes. Carboxylic acids can form both hydrogen bonds and dimers, which need more energy input to break apart, and hence have the highest boiling points in the series.

b Increasing number of carbon atoms means increasing molecular weight and increasing intermolecular forces in the non-polar sections of each molecule in the series. This leads to increased boiling points.

7

<table>
<tr><td>Propan-2-ol</td><td><pre>
    H   H   H
    | | |
H — C — C — C — H
    | | |
    H   O   H
        |
        H
</pre></td></tr>
<tr><td>Hexanoic acid</td><td><pre>
    H   H   H   H   H
    | | | | | O
H — C — C — C — C — C — C //
    | | | | | \
    H   H   H   H   H   O — H
</pre></td></tr>
<tr><td>Hept-3-yne</td><td><pre>
    H   H   H   H   H
    | | | | |
H — C — C — C ≡ C — C — C — C — H
    | | | | |
    H   H   H   H   H
</pre></td></tr>
<tr><td>1,1, 1-Trifluoroethane</td><td><pre>
    F   H
    | |
F — C — C — H
    | |
    F   H
</pre></td></tr>
<tr><td>Heptan-3-ol</td><td><pre>
    H   H   OH H   H   H   H
    | | | | | | |
H — C — C — C — C — C — C — C — H
    | | | | | | |
    H   H   H   H   H   H   H
</pre></td></tr>
<tr><td>2-Chloro-2,5-dibromo-3-methyl-hept-3-ene</td><td><pre>
    H   Cl H   H   Br H   H
    | | | | | | |
H — C — C — C = C — C — C — C — H
    | | | | | |
    H   Br CH3   H   H   H
</pre></td></tr>
</table>

8 Hexane and hexene are large non-polar molecules with non-polar covalent bonds, governed by dispersion forces, so they have no affinity or attraction for polar water molecules.

Ethanol and propanoic acid have polar functional groups on each molecule, they are polar molecules, and they are attracted to polar water molecules by forming hydrogen bonds.

9 a **i** Molecule 1: 1 chiral carbon atom

ii Molecule 2: 2 chiral carbon atoms

iii Molecule 3: 1 chiral carbon atom

b **i** Pair 1 are enantiomers.

ii Pair 2 are the same compound.

iii Pair 3 are enantiomers.

Heptane	2-Methylhexane	3-Methylhexane
C—C—C—C—C—C—C	C | C—C—C—C—C—C	C | C—C—C—C—C—C
2,2-Dimethylpentane	**2,3-Dimethylpentane**	**2,4-Dimethylpentane**
C | C—C—C—C—C | C	C | C—C—C—C—C | C	C C | | C—C—C—C—C
3,3-Dimethylpentane	**3-Ethylpentane**	**2,2,3-Trimethylbutane**
C | C—C—C—C—C | C	C—C | C—C—C—C—C	C | C—C—C—C | | C C

Chapter 10

RESEARCH REVIEW 10

1 Green polymers, renewable resources, ecological footprint, synthetic polymers.

2 Green polymer = polymer produced from waste products through recycling and reuse

Renewable resources = replaceable at a rate equal to or greater than the rate of use

Ecological footprint = human requirements on Earth

Synthetic polymers = polymers made by chemical synthesis

3 Student answers will vary depending on each student's question. Guidance is provided below. Student questions should consider the following:

- the definition of a polymer
- types of polymers; those found in nature compared with synthetic polymers made from fossil fuels
- a summary of recent developments for the production of more sustainable polymers
- advantages and disadvantages of the use of synthetic versus green, polymers, including extent of biodegradability and environmental impacts.

EXAM EXCELLENCE 10

1 A **2** D **3** B **4** A **5** C

6 a $CH_3CHClCH_3(l) + NH_3(g) \rightarrow CH_3C_2H_3(l) + NH_4Cl(aq)$

b Prop-2-amine

7

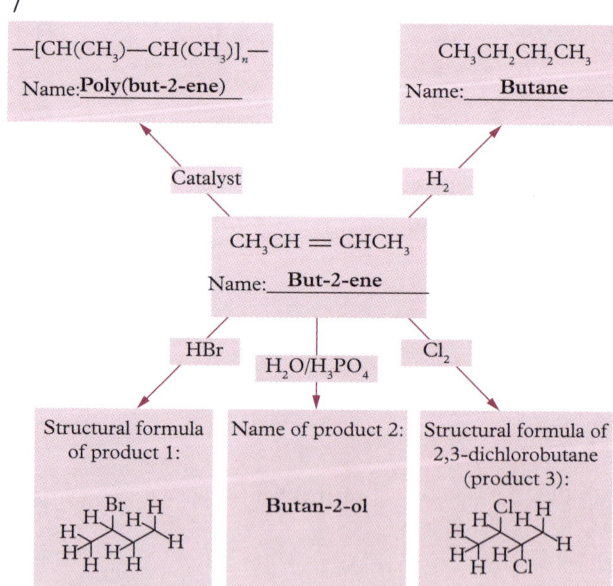

8 a $2CH_3CH_2CH_2CH_3(g) + 13O_2(g) \rightarrow 8CO_2(g) + 10H_2O(g)$

b $CH_3CH{=}CHCH_3(l) + HBr(l) \rightarrow CH_3CH_2{-}CHBrCH_3(l)$

9 a Tetrafluoroethene (monomer) and polytetrafluoroethene (polymer).

b Addition polymerisation

10

$CH_2{=}CH_2$ (Ethene) $\xrightarrow[\text{Catalyst}]{H_2O}$ CH_3CH_2OH (Ethanol)

$CH_3CH_2CH_3$ (Propane) $\xrightarrow[\text{UV light}]{Cl_2}$ $CH_3CH_2CH_2Cl$ (1-Chloropropane) $\xrightarrow{NaOH}$ $CH_3CH_2CH_2OH$ (Propan-1-ol) $\xrightarrow[H^+]{Cr_2O_7^{2-}}$ CH_3CH_2COOH (Propanoic acid)

Ethanol + Propanoic acid $\xrightarrow{H_2SO_4}$ $CH_3CH_2COOCH_2CH_3$ (Ethyl propanoate)

Chapter 11

RESEARCH REVIEW 11

1 Question 2 is stronger because it is researchable, not too vague or too specific, measurable, does not have a yes/no answer, and is focused on one organic compound.

2 Steps should include conducting research from credible sources, analyse data to identify evidence for the question, identify trends in the data, identify limitations, interpret evidence and construct a scientific argument, draft a report and draw conclusions relating to the research question.

EXAM EXCELLENCE 11

1 C **2** A **3** A **4** B **5** B

6

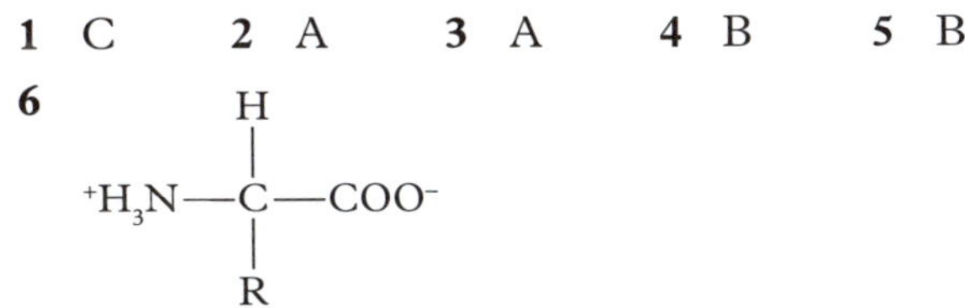

7 Enzymes are biological catalysts and operate 10^{10} times faster than inorganic catalysts. Enzymes operate under optimum conditions, whereas inorganic catalysts operate under high temperatures and pressures.

8 Primary: linear chain sequence of amino acids joined by peptide bonds.

Secondary: localised folding to an α-helix or a β-pleated sheet; held in place by hydrogen bonding between C=O of one peptide bond and the amino hydrogen atom of another peptide bond.

9 Disaccharides

10 Saponification reaction:

CH_2—O—C(=O)$(CH_2)_{14}CH_3$
CH—O—C(=O)$(CH_2)_{14}CH_3$ + 3 NaOH
CH_2—O—C(=O)$(CH_2)_{14}CH_3$

A fat + 3 NaOH Sodium hydroxide (or KOH, potassium hydroxide)

↓ Saponification

CH_2—OH
CH—OH
CH_2—OH
+ 3 $CH_3(CH_2)_{14}CO_2Na$

Glycerol + A crude soap

Chapter 12

RESEARCH REVIEW 12

Student answers will vary depending on each student's resources. Guidance is provided below.

Resources should be based on one analytical technique for one industry.

For guidance on credible and non-credible resources, refer to Research review 1 answers.

EXAM EXCELLENCE 12

1 A 2 D 3 B 4 C 5 A

6 67608 kDa

7 $C_3H_6O_2$

8

m/z ratio	29	45	73	74
Species	$C_2H_5^+$	$COOH^+$	$C_3H_5O_2^+$	$C_3H_6O_2^+$

9 Molecular formula is the empirical formula from mass spectrum data (i.e. $C_3H_6O_2$).

10

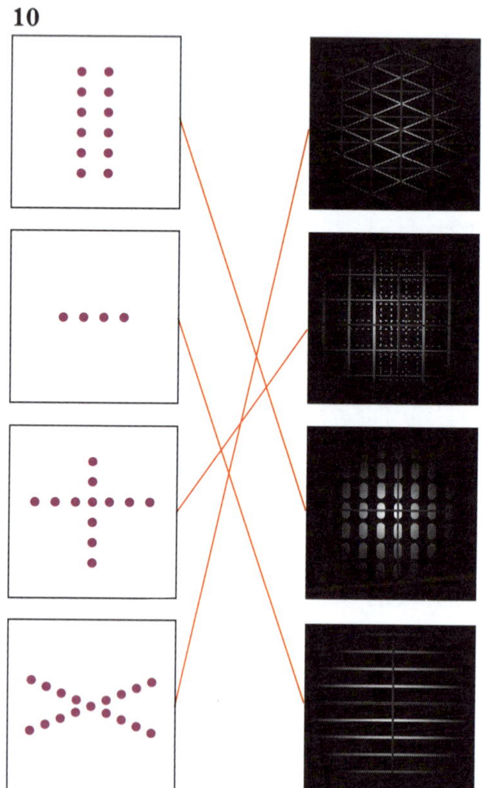

Chapter 13

RESEARCH REVIEW 13

Student answers will vary depending on each student's resources. For guidance on referencing, refer to Research review 2. An example answer is provided below.

In-text citation: (Rathnayake et al., 2012)

Reference list: Rathnayake, W.G.I.U., Ismail, H., Baharin, A., Darsanasiri, A.G.N.D. and Rajapakse, S., 2012, Synthesis and characterization of nano silver based natural rubber latex foam for imparting antibacterial and anti-fungal properties, Polymer Testing, 31, 5, 586–592.

EXAM EXCELLENCE 13

1 D 2 B 3 D 4 B 5 A

6 a Anode: $H_2(g) + 2OH^-(aq) \rightarrow 2H_2O(l) + 2e^-$

Cathode: $O_2(g) + 2H_2O(l) + 4e^- \rightarrow 4OH^-(aq)$

b To conduct electricity and to act as a catalyst.

7 a $CaO(s) + H_2O(l) \rightarrow Ca(OH)_2(aq)$

b 30% (29.63%)

8 a $2Al(s) + 3I_2(s) \rightarrow 2AlI_3(s)$

b 5.4 g (5.354 g)

9 $CaO(s) + 2NH_4Cl(s) \rightarrow$
$CaCl_2(s) + H_2O(g) + 2NH_3(g)$

10 A high temperature is required for a fast reaction rate and a low temperature is required for a high (equilibrium) yield because it is an exothermic reaction. The compromise is that a moderate temperature is used with a catalyst.

Chapter 14

RESEARCH REVIEW 14

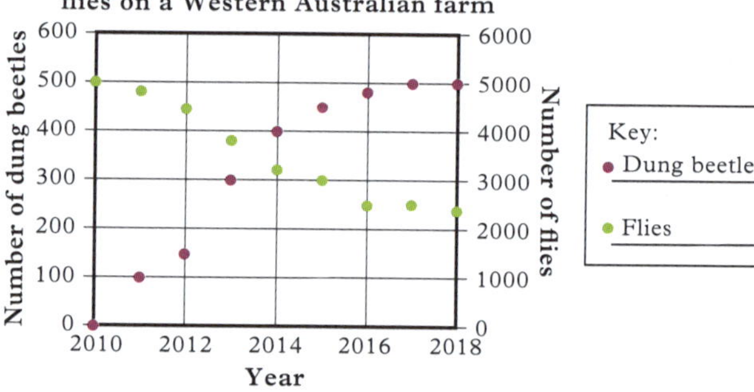

The increase in dung beetles is proportional to the decrease in flies. In 2010, the Western Australian farm had a pest problem with 5000 flies. In 2011, the farm introduced dung beetles and flies started to decrease in numbers. In 2018, there were 500 dung beetles and flies were down to 2400.

EXAM EXCELLENCE 14

1 A 2 C 3 A 4 C 5 A

6 A method for tracking atoms in a reaction; for calculating the mass of atoms of reactants used to form products (as a percentage).

7 $C(s) + 2H_2O(g) \rightarrow CO_2(g) + 2H_2(g)$

Atom economy is 8.4%.

8 Living or recently living matter used as a fuel source.

9 % yield = actual yield/theoretical yield × 100%

10 Water electrolysis: 88.8%

Decomposition of hydrogen peroxide: 47.0%

Chapter 15

RESEARCH REVIEW 15

1 So far, there are only few studies dealing with arsenic (As) removal from groundwater using chitin or chitosan and no evidence of the use of these natural polymers for arsenic trioxide (As_2O_3) delivery in tumor therapy.

2 Chitin and/or chitosan might have the right properties to be employed as efficient polymers for arsenic trioxide (As_2O_3) delivery in tumor therapy.

3 Da Sacco, L. and Masotti A., 2010, Chitin and chitosan as multipurpose natural polymers for groundwater arsenic removal and As_2O_3 delivery in tumor therapy, Marine Drugs, 8, 5, 1518–1525.

EXAM EXCELLENCE 15

1 D 2 B 3 B 4 C 5 B

6 H, Cl / C=C / H, H

7 a Carbohydrates (or saccharides).

b Starch or glycogen.

8 NH_2^+ COOH

9 a The compound contains a double or triple carbon–carbon bond.

b H, H / C=C / H, H

10 CH3 H O H C C N C—N C O H H H CH2 OH OH

Chapter 16

RESEARCH REVIEW 16

1 Student answers will vary depending on each student's question. Guidance is provided here. Student questions should consider the following:

- the definition of nanomolecular manufacturing and nanotechnology
- bottom-up, top-down and self-assembly
- the effect of working with specific material properties at a nanomolecular or atomic scale
- time taken to construct one or specific products with improved technology at a nanomolecular or atomic scale compared with that of conventional manufacturing methods
- possible health and safety risks of working with materials at a nanomolecular or atomic scale.

2 A large number of websites on nanomolecular manufacturing are not credible resources as this topic is a new scientific field. This means there are a lot of websites filled with opinions and not scientific facts. These websites can be useful for finding the scientific articles that are credible.

3 Lack of scientific articles, many futuristic sci-fi distraction websites, current science is still being published and only conference proceedings are available.

EXAM EXCELLENCE 16

1 C 2 B 3 B 4 A 5 D

6 a 5×10^7 nm

b 1.2×10^7 nm

c 2×10^{12} nm

7 Two properties from the following list: different optical properties, no effect of Brownian motion and/or gravitational forces compared with small particles, electrical conductivity compared with limited electrical conductivity for smaller particles, decreased surface-area-to-volume ratio of larger particles that affect reactivity and reaction rates, and electromagnetic forces compared with that of smaller-sized molecular particles or nanoparticles.

8 • Bottom-up: building nanomolecular structures atom by atom by using a scanning tunnelling microscope.
• Top-down: small-scale versions of machines used to cut and shape structures into nanomolecular-sized pieces, by a micro-etching process.
• Self-assembly: nanomolecular atoms and molecules put themselves together, which naturally occurs in biological processes like the manufacture of proteins, cell membranes and other cellular-level processes.

9 The scanning tunnelling microscope (STM) works by producing a flow of electrical current that occurs between the tip of the microscope probe and the surface of the nanomolecular object. The variation in strength of this current due to the shape of the surface is used to form an image.

10 Nano-sized molecular particles would have a very large surface area for a given volume. The larger the surface area, the more molecules that can be adsorbed, increasing the reaction rate and therefore being a more effective catalyst.

Unit 4 Practice assessment

RESEARCH INVESTIGATION

Student answers will vary depending on each student's research question and resources.

A sample research question is: 'To what extent can the Queensland Government support the production of biofuels?'

Resources should include information on biofuel production in Queensland and other states as a way to compare and show where Queensland could potentially support additional biofuel production.